Contents

Camino Elevation Profile — 1

The Camino Francés — 4

Basque Country & Navarra, 162.4km
- 1: St. Jean to Roncesvalles, 24.7km……4
- 2: Roncesvalles to Zubiri, 21.9km………8
- 3: Zubiri to Pamplona, 20.6km…………10
- 4: Pamplona to Puente la Reina, 24.1km…………………………………14
- 5: Puente la Reina to Estella, 22.0km..16
- 6: Estella to Los Arcos, 21.6km…………20
- 7: Los Arcos to Logroño, 27.5km………22

La Rioja & Castilla y León, 122.9km
- 8: Logroño to Nájera, 29.8km…………26
- 9: Nájera to Santo Domingo, 20.9km..28
- 10: Santo Domingo to Belorado, 22.3km…………………………………30
- 11: Belorado to Agés, 27.5km…………32
- 12: Agés to Burgos, 22.4km……………34

Meseta, 233.1km
- 13: Burgos to Hontanas, 31.3km………38
- 14: Hontanas to Boadilla, 28.4km……40
- 15: Boadilla to Carrión, 24.7km………42
- 16: Carrión to Terradillos, 26.5km………44
- 17: Terradillos to Calzadilla, 26.5km……46
- 18: Calzadilla to Mansilla, 23.8km………50
- 19: Mansilla to León, 18.1km……………52
- 20: León to Villar de Mazarife, 22.0km…56
- 21: V/de Mazarife to Astorga, 31.5km……58

Cantabrian Mtns. & El Bierzo, 101.2km
- 22: Astorga to Foncebadón, 26.0km………60
- 23: Foncebadón to Ponferrada, 27.1km…62
- 24: Ponferrada to Villafranca, 24.4km……64
- 25: Villafranca to La Faba, 23.8km………66

Galicia, 159.2km
- 26: La Faba to Triacastela, 25.5km………70
- 27: Triacastela to Barbadelo, 22.5km……74
- 28: Barbadelo to Hospital Alta da Cruz, 29.9km…………………………………78
- 29: Hospital Alta da Cruz to Melide, 28.1km…………………………………82
- 30: Melide to Arca, 33.0km………………86
- 31: Arca to Santiago, 20.2km……………90

About the Authors — 96

Legend — 97

Ride with GPS mobile phone offline navigation and GPX track downloads

More information and booking links at
www.caminoguidebook.com

1

ST-JEAN-PIED-DE-PORT TO RONCESVALLES

24.7km (15.3mi), ▲ 1332M / ▼ 571M, ⊕ 7-9 Hours
🅿 61%, 15.1km, 🆄 39%, 9.6km, **Difficulty:** ▄▄ ▟

💡 The Camino Francés traditionally begins in St-Jean-Pied-de-Port, which can be reached by public transport by train or bus 🗗. This path crosses the Pyrenees on the first day of its journey from France into Spain. Various Camino routes in France converge on this historic town, channeling hikers onto one route, the Camino Francés, or the "French Way." Two-thirds of pilgrims arriving in Santiago walk the Camino Francés, of which 15% start their journey here. ⚠ The recommended Napoleon route is closed in winter and bad weather. The alternate Valcarlos route (1A) has less climbing and more pavement.

0.0 St-Jean-Pied-de-Port 🅰 🄷 🍴🛒⊙⊕€ⓘ▲🚌, See p. 6.

5.3 Honto 🄷
🄷 **Ferme Ithurburia** (€92/104): 🍴🅆🄳, ☏0559371117 🗗

7.7 Orisson 🅰 🄷 🍴 Book lodging in advance!
🅰 🄷 **Refuge Orisson** (🛏28, €45/-/114 🍴): 🍴🅆🄳⊙, ☏0681497956 🗗, ⊙Mar-Oct
🅰 🄷 **Aubergue Borda** (🛏12, €45/-/114 🍴): 🍴🅆🄳⊙, ☏661929743 🗗,
⊙Apr-Oct, 900m after Orisson

24.7 Roncesvalles 🅰 🄷 🍴🛒 🅸
1. 🅰 **Municipal** (🛏183, €14): 🍴🅆🄳🛜, ☏948760000 🗗, reservations ⊙2pm all year
2. 🄷 **Casa Sabina** (€58/65): 🍴, ☏948760012 🗗
3. 🄷 **La Posada** (€83/100): 🍴, ☏948760225 🗗
4. 🄷 **Hotel Roncesvalles/Casa de Beneficiados** (€89/107): 🍴🅆🄳🛜, ☏948760105 🗗, option of apartment with kitchenette

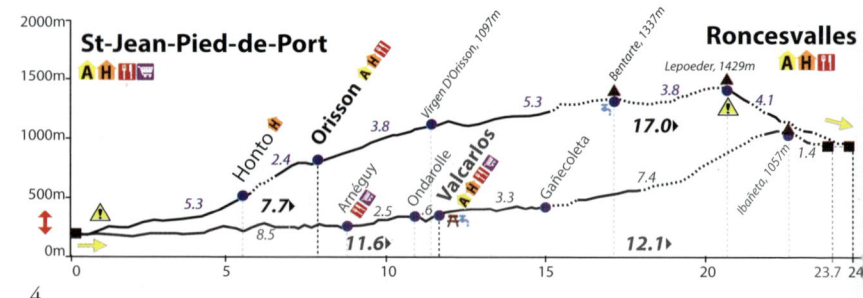

4

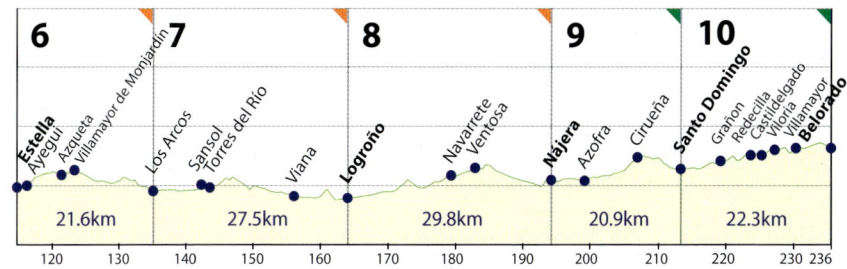

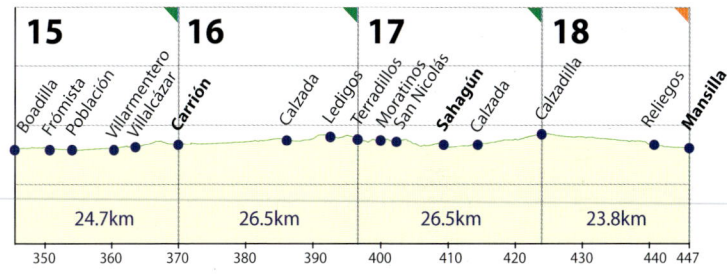

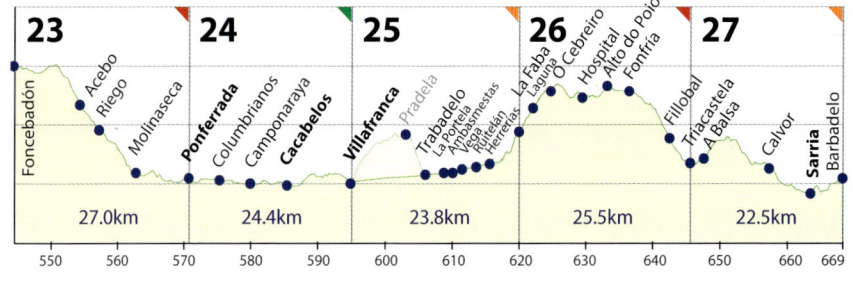

Towns listed on elevation tables have albergues. There are additional private accommodations in towns not listed (see stage chapters for details). Bolded towns have a population of at least 1,000.

CAMINO DE SANTIAGO: CAMINO FRANCÉS

Camino de Santiago Maps: Camino Francés: St. Jean - Santiago
2nd edition, January 2025
Copyright © 2013-2025 Village to Village Press, LLC

Village to Village Press, LLC, Harrisonburg, VA, USA
www.villagetovillagepress.com

Photographs/Diagrams
All photographs and diagrams © David Landis and Anna Dintaman

Cover Photographs © David Landis
Front: Stage 1 from St-Jean-Pied-de-Port to Roncesvalles
Back (left to right): Reaching Castrojeriz, Santiago Cathedral, Arrow after Santa Catalina

ISBN: 978-1-947474-28-4
Library of Congress Control Number: 2018909560

Text, photographs, images and diagrams © Village to Village Press, LLC, 2025
Village to Village® is a registered trademark of Village to Village Press, LLC.
Map data based on openstreetmap.org, © OpenStreetMap contributors
Cover and book design by David Landis

All rights reserved. No part of this publication may be reproduced, stored in a retrieval system or transmitted in any form or any means, digital, electronic, mechanical, photocopying, recording or otherwise, except brief extracts for the purpose of review, without the written permission of the authors.

Disclaimer: *Every reasonable effort has been made to ensure that the information contained in this book is accurate. However, no guarantee is made regarding its accuracy or completeness. Reader assumes responsibility and liability for all actions in relation to using the provided information, including if actions result in injury, death, loss or damage of personal property or other complications.*

Note about town names: We generally use the Spanish name for cities and towns, though most also have a name or spelling in the local language. We occasionally use the local language name when it is the most prominent.

This **map guidebook** is designed to be lightweight and minimalist. It provides stage and city maps, lodging, services, and basic tips ☼. This book does not include travel preparation and packing information, comprehensive route descriptions, extensive historical background information, nor all hotel listings. A comprehensive 288-page guidebook to the Camino Francés is also available by Village to Village Press.

For comprehensive **planning information**, visit www.caminoguidebook.com

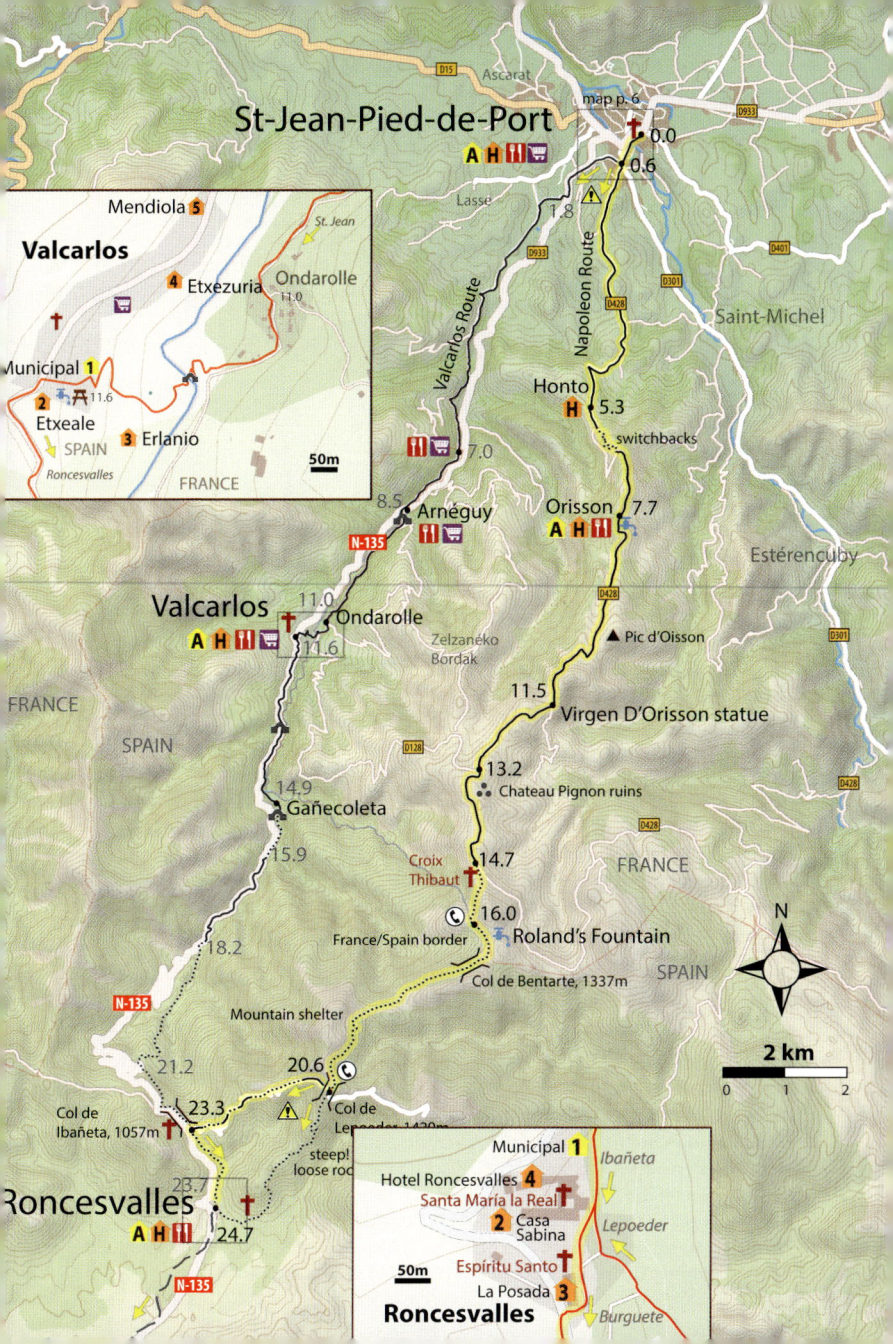

0.0 St-Jean-Pied-de-Port A H 🍴 🛒 🚲 ⊕ ✚ 🅸 ⛺ 🚌 ♿

1. **A H Municipal** (🛏32, €12/-/30 🍳): 🐕 W D ⊕, Citadelle 55, ☎0559370509 📧, ⊕2pm all year
2. **A Porte Saint-Jacques** (🛏6, €29 🍳): 🐕 🎧, Citadelle 51, ☎630997561 📧, ⊕Mar-Oct
3. **A H Makila** (🛏12, €27-30/-/80 🍳): 🐕 W D 🎧⊕, Citadelle 35, ⊕May-Oct
4. **A H Esteban Etxea** (🛏12, €22/55/66): 🍴 W D, 29 la Citadelle, ☎638228005 📧, ⊕Feb-Nov
5. **A H La Vita è Bella** (🛏13, €19/-/42 🍳): 🍴 🎧, 4 Place du Trinquet, ☎768234007 📧
6. **A H Izaxulo** (🛏18, €22/-/75): W D 🎧⊕, Renaud 2, ☎0524341900 📧, ⊕Mar-Oct
7. **A ⭐ Beilari** (🛏14, €43 🍳🍴): 🐕⊕, Citadelle 40, ☎0559372468 📧, ⊕Mar-Oct
8. **A H Le Lièvre et La Tortue** (🛏15, €23/-/70): 🍴 W D 🎧⊕, Citadelle 30, ☎0663629235 📧, ⊕all y
9. **A H Gîte Ultreïa** (🛏15, €25/-/60): 🐕 W D 🎧⊕, Citadelle 8, ☎0680884622 📧, ⊕May-Oct 15
10. **A H Compostella** (🛏13, €25/-/65): 🎧⊕, D'Arneguy 6, ☎0559370236 📧, ⊕Mar 15-Oct 10
11. **A H Bidean** (🛏12, €20/-/50): 🍴 🎧, Espagne 11, ☎670296666 📧, ⊕all year
12. **A Chemin Vers L'Etoile** (🛏46, €20-23 🍳): 🍴 W D 🎧, Espagne 21, ☎0559372071 📧, ⊕Mar-Oc
13. **A Kaserna** (par, 🛏14, €25 🍳🍴): Espagne 43, ☎0559376517 📧, ⊕2pm May-Oct
14. **A H Zuharpeta** (🛏22, €22/-/62): 🍴 🎧⊕, Zuharpeta 5, ☎0559373588 📧, ⊕Mar 15-Oct 15
15. **A H La Coquille Napoléon** (🛏10, €20/-/60): 🍴 🎧, Uhart-Cize, ☎0662259940 📧, ⊕a.y., 1.4k
16. **H Villa Esponda** (€80-120): 🐕 W 🎧, Place du Trinquet 9, ☎0679075252 📧, ⊕all year, room for
17. **H Itzalpea** (€89/128): 🍴 🎧, Place du Trinquet 5, ☎0559370366 📧
18. **H Hôtel Ramuntcho** (€100/112): 🍴 🎧, Citadelle 24, ☎0559373517 📧, Old City
19. **H Hôtel des Pyrénées** (€185-205): 🍴 🎧, Place du General-de-Gaulle 19, ☎0559370101
20. **H Maison Donamaria** (€80/95): 🛏, d'Olhonce 1, ☎0661902921 📧
21. **H Gure Lana** (€70-90 🍳): 🎧, Caro 8, ☎0524341497 📧
22. **H Zazpiak-Bat** (€75): 🍴 W D ⊕, 13b Maréchal Harispe, ☎658626636, 900m into route
▲ **Municipal Campsite** (tent €12): Aronton, ☎0559371119 📧, ⊕Apr-Oct

View of Valcarlos

⚠ Alternate Stage 1A: Valcarlos Route
St. Jean to Roncesvalles (via Valcarlos), 23.7km

🅿 70%, 16.6km, 🆄 30%, 7.1km

💡 In spite of the sections of highway walking, much of this route is on pleasant quiet country roads or lovely dirt footpaths. The trail crisscrosses the Nive River and Spanish/French border. Remain vigilant for vehicles on blind corners, as this highway has no shoulder in most places.

11.6 Valcarlos A H 🍴 🛒 ➕ € ℹ 🚏
1. **A Municipal** (🛏24, €15 🎒): 🏧 Ⓦ 📶, Elizaldea 52, ☎696231809 ↗, 🕛12pm all year, key may be at municipal building
2. **H Pensión Etxeale** (€60-65): 🍴 📶, Elizalde 8, ☎690842264
3. **H Casa Erlanio** (€45/55): 💳 📶, Elizaldea 58, ☎948790218
4. **H Casa Zigabo Etxezuria** (€55): 📶, Elizaldea 60, ☎948790011 ↗
5. **H Apartamentos Mendiola** (€80-100): 💳 📶, Elizaldea 138, ☎609755105 ↗

24.0 Roncesvalles A H 🍴 🛒 ℹ 🚏, *See p. 4-5.*

2

RONCESVALLES TO ZUBIRI

21.9km (13.6mi), ▲ 315M / ▼ 735M, ⊙ 5-6 Hours
℗ 23%, 5.0 km, Ⓤ 77%, 16.9 km, **Difficulty:**

☀ This is a beautiful day of walking, primarily on forest walking trails, occasionally crossing the main highway. Be prepared for lots of up and down on rocky surfaces; save energy for the steep descent into Zubiri. Periodic services in charming towns pleasantly break up the stage.

3.0 Burguete
- **Lorentx Aterpea** (🛏42, €15-18): , San Nicolas 56, ☏623286129, ⊙a.y.
- **Casa Pedroarena** (€45/50): , ☏948760164
- **Loizu** (€70/76): , S. Nicolás 13, ☏948760008
- **Don Jáuregui de Burguete** (€60): San Nicolás 32, ☏948760031
- **Casa Bergara** (€50): , San Nicolás 44, ☏948760044
- **Hostal Burguete** (€40/60): , S. Nicolas 71, ☏948760005
- **Txikipolit** (€25/pilgrim): , Roncesvalles 42, ☏948760019

6.7 Espinal
- **Irugoienea** (🛏22, €15/-/45): , Oihanilum 2, ☏649412487, ⊙Apr-Oct
- **Haizea** (🛏30, €15/-/75): , Saroiberri 2, ☏948760379, ⊙Apr-Oct
- **Casa Patxikuzuria** (€36/40): , Errekazabal 21, ☏948760167
- **Camping Urrobi** (🛏42, €13.50/-/115): , ☏948760200, ⊙Apr-Oct, +1.5km

11.8 Gerendiain
- **Casa Rural Lastur y Rey** (€20/pilgrim): , San Pedro 8 & 72, ☏679270519
- **La Posada Nueva** (€35/55): , San Pedro 2, ☏699131433
- **Casa Batit** (€41-50/46-55): , San Pedro 18A, ☏616068347
- **Maitetxu** (€45-55/55-65): , San Pedro 58A, ☏669755563

13.6 Linzoain
- **Posada El Camino** (€22/44/44 pilgrim rate): , San Saturnino 48, ☏622688535, ⊙Apr-Oct

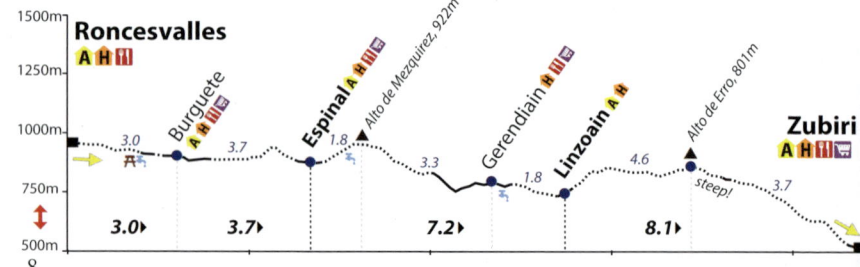

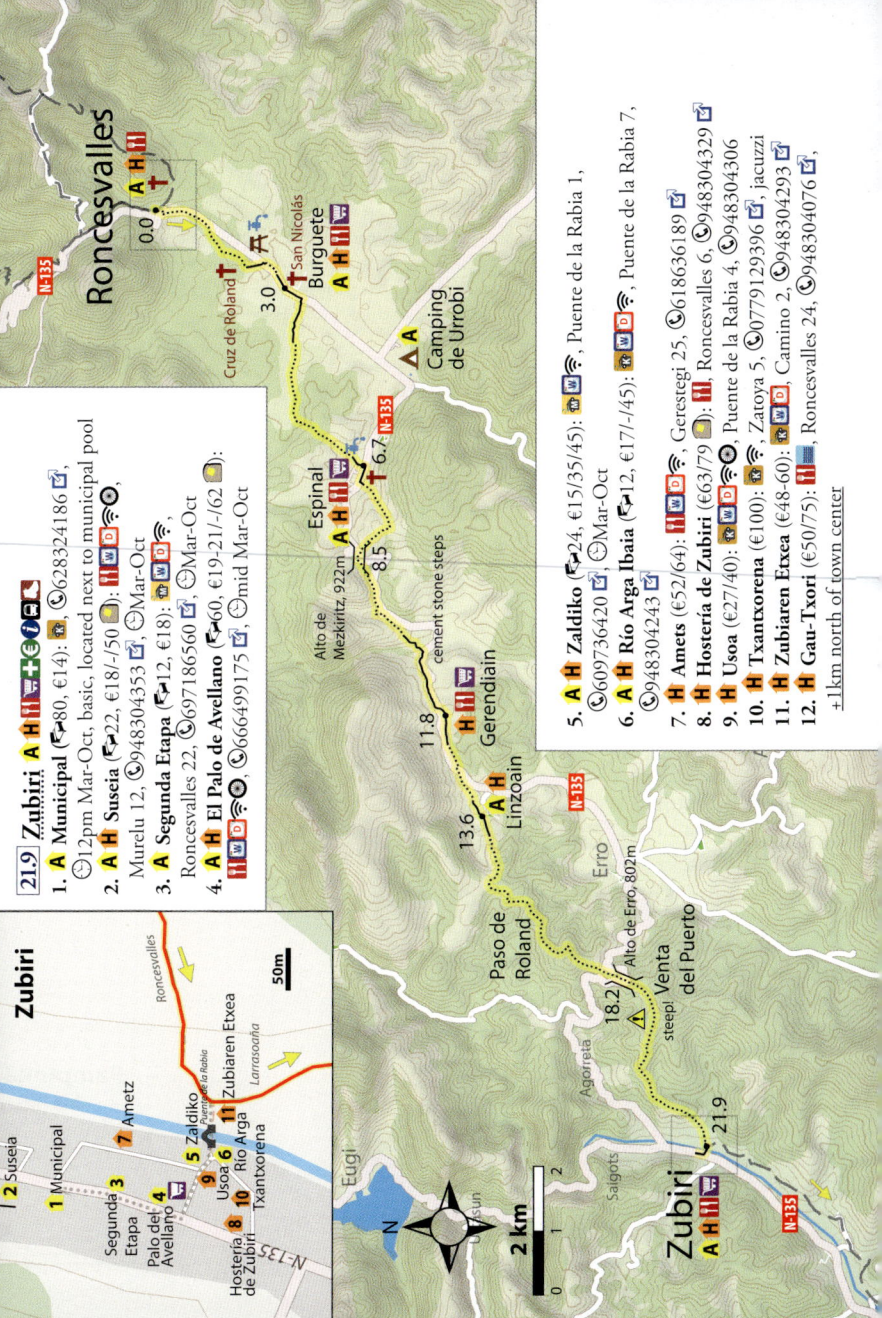

21.9 Zubiri

1. **Municipal** (☎628324186, €80, €14); 12pm Mar-Oct, basic, located next to municipal pool
2. **Suseia** (☎22, €18/-/50); 948304353, Mar-Oct
3. **Segunda Etapa** (☎12, €18); Roncesvalles 22, 697186560, Mar-Oct
4. **El Palo de Avellano** (☎60, €19-21/-/62); 666499175, mid Mar-Oct
5. **Zaldiko** (☎24, €15/35/45); 609736420, Mar-Oct
6. **Rio Arga Ibaia** (☎12, €17/-/45); Puente de la Rabia 7, 948304243
7. **Amets** (€52/64); Gerestegi 25, 618636189
8. **Hostería de Zubiri** (€63/79); Puente de la Rabia 1, Roncesvalles 6, 948304329
9. **Usoa** (€27/40); Puente de la Rabia 4, 948304306
10. **Txantxorena** (€100); Zatoya 5, 0779129396, jacuzzi
11. **Zubiaren Exea** (€48-60); Camino 2, 948304293
12. **Gau-Txori** (€50/75); Roncesvalles 24, 948304076, ±1km north of town center

3

ZUBIRI TO PAMPLONA

20.6km (12.8mi), ▲ 288M / ▼ 359M, ⏱ 5-6 Hours
🅿 44%, 9.1km, Ⓤ 56%, 11.5km, **Difficulty:** ▪️▫️▫️

☀️ Today's path primarily follows the Arga River through rural hamlets on pleasant natural paths with plenty of places to fill water. The day ends in Pamplona, the largest city by population on the Camino Francés. Some urban road walking towards the end leads to the charming walled Old City, alive with cafés and Hemingway lore.

3.7 Urdániz A, +500m
- **A Acá y Allá** (6, €20): San Miguel 18, ☎615257666, +500m

5.7 Larrasoaña A H 🍴🛒
1. **A Municipal** (36, €10): San Nicolás, ☎605505489, ⏱1:30pm mid Mar-Oct
2. **A San Nicolás** (40, €15-18): Sorandi 5-7, ☎619559225, ⏱12pm Mar-Oct
3. **H Pensión Tau** (€75): Errotabidea 18, ☎948304720
4. **H El Peregrino** (€50-70): San Nicolás 50, ☎948304554

6.4 Akerreta H
- **H Akerreta** (€100/128): Transfiguración 11, ☎948304572, makes an appearance in the film *The Way*

9.5 Zuriáin A 🍴
- **A Parada de Zuriáin** (16, €15/40/70): Landa 8, ☎699556741, ⏱Mar-Oct

12.7 Zabaldica A
- **A ⭐ Zabaldika** (par, 18, don): San Esteban 8, ☎948330918, ⏱Apr 15- Oct 15, welcoming, communal meals and pilgrim blessing

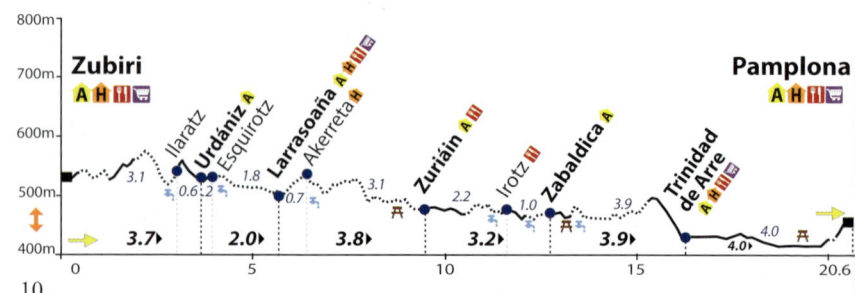

10

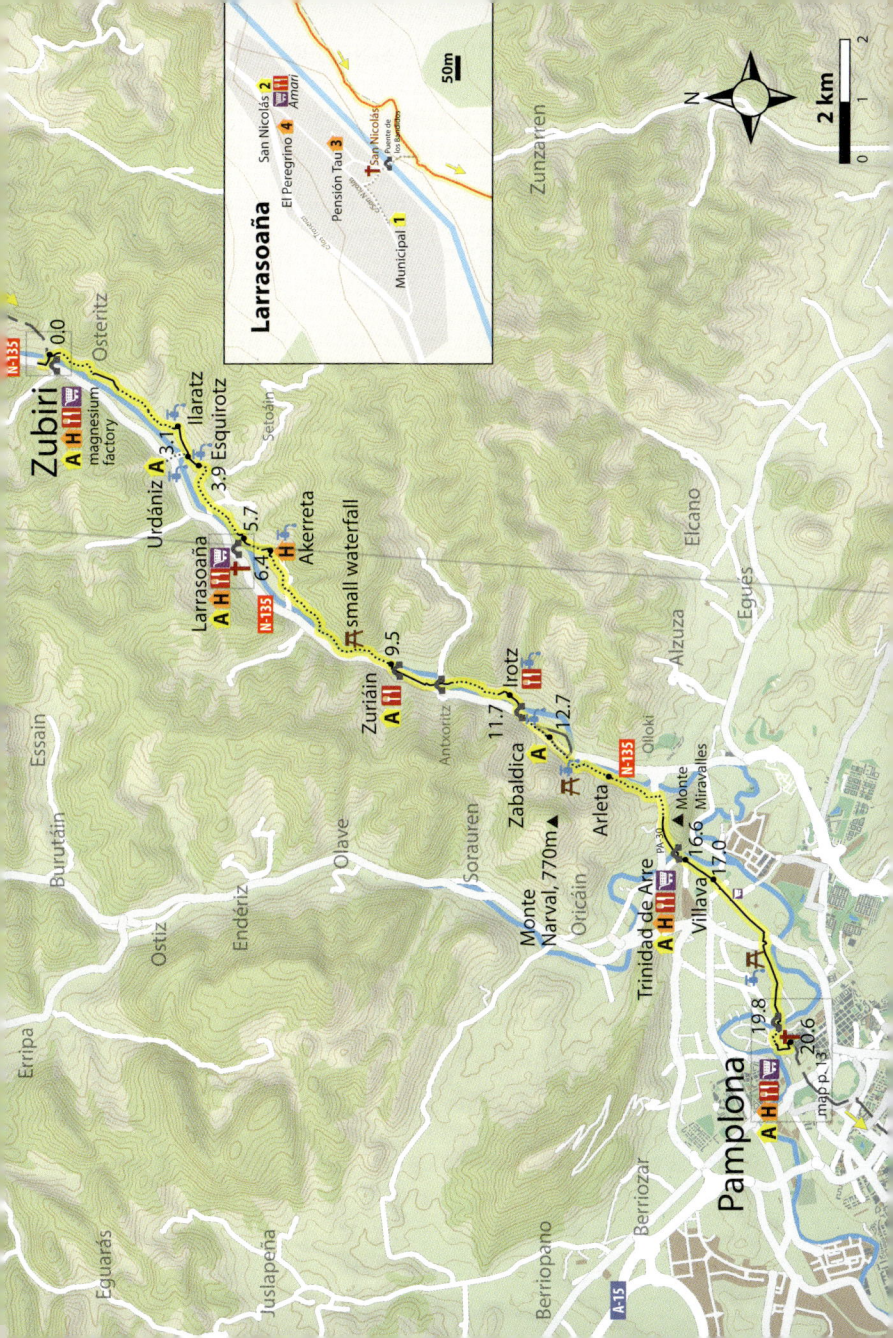

CAMINO DE SANTIAGO: CAMINO FRANCÉS

16.6 Trinidad de Arre/Villava A H 🍴 🛒 ✚ ℹ️ 🚌

A Trinidad de Arre (par, 🛏34, €10): 🔑 W D ⊙, at the bridge, ☎948332941 📧, 🕐all year (call in winter), historical pilgrim hostel, daily mass

A Villava Municipal (🛏54, €15): 🍴🔑 W D 📶 ⊙, Pedro de Atarrabia 17-19, ☎948517731 📧, 🕐mid Mar-Oct, access spa & gym €3.50

H Villava (€50/60): 🍴📶, ☎948333676 📧

H Pensión Obel (€32/42): 🍴📶, Las Eras 5, ☎651802499

20.6 Pamplona

is the first major city on the Camino and a worthwhile place to take a rest day if you enjoy exploring historic buildings, twisting Old City alleys, and expansive green parks. 💡 If there are any items in your backpack that you haven't used yet (except rain gear & first aid kit), consider mailing them ahead

Pamplona is best known for the **running of the bulls** at the 📅 **Fiesta de San Fermín**, celebrated July 6-14 each year, in which six bulls are released daily to run a course through the city to the plaza. The festival was propelled to worldwide fame by its prominence in Hemingway's The *Sun Also Rises*. Now, locals and tourists come to run with the bulls while consuming copious amounts of wine (an estimated three million liters are imbibed during the festivities), precipitating numerous injuries. The city swells with over a million people, accommodations rates quadruple, and albergues close. If you happen to pass through Pamplona during San Fermínes, just keep on walking (or run!) and look for a bed in the next town.

Pamplona was founded by the Roman general Pompeoalo, built over a previous Basque encampment, an ideal defensible location along the *Via Trajana*. Roman ruins have been excavated from under the **cathedral**, including 1st-century streets and buildings. Muslims took the city in 718 and ruled until overthrown by local Basques in 799. In 778, Charlemagne was said to have destroyed the city walls of Pamplona, leading up to the Battle of Roncesvalles.

An influx of foreign immigrants in the 12th century led to infighting between neighborhoods, with each ethnic neighborhood fortifying themselves against the others. Pamplona was more fort than city, encapsulated within the defensive walls until the 20th century when building was finally allowed outside city walls. Today, Pamplona is a prosperous and attractive city with a number of historical buildings and museums. Plaza del Castillo is a great place for an evening stroll, with numerous cafés including Café Iruña, a favorite haunt of Hemingway, and historic hotels such as La Perla, which has hosted Orson Welles, Charlie Chaplin, and Hemingway.

0.6 Pamplona A H 🏠 🛒 ⚕ ➕ ℹ 🅿 🚌 🚉 Pop. 197,932, 📖 Named for Roman general Pompaelo, Basque: *Iruña* "the city," ℹ S. Saturnino 2, ☎948420700; 🕘 9am-2pm, 3-5pm, Caminoteca, Curia 5, ☎948210316, 🕘Apr-Oct 8am-9pm; all San Fermín prices higher

A Jesús y María (muni, 🛏112, €11): ♿ W D, Compañía 4, ☎948222644, 🕘all year

A Casa Ibarrola (🛏20, €20 🧺): ♿ W D 📶 ⚕, Carmen 31, ☎692208463 📱, 🕘all year

A H Pamplona-Iruñako (🛏24, €20/-/41): ♿ W D 📶 ⚕, Carmen 18, ☎685735595 📱, 🕘Feb-Nov

A H Plaza Catedral (🛏46, €17-20/-/60): ♿ W D 📶, Navarrería 35, ☎620913968 📱, 🕘all year

A Jacobusfreunde Paderborn (asoc, 🛏24, €10): W D 📶, Playa de Caparroso 6, ☎948211712 📱, 🕘Mar-Oct, riverside albergue run by a German confraternity

A Betania (par, 🛏beds, don): 🍴 🧺 by donation, Recoletas 1, 🕘Apr-Oct 2pm

A H Aloha Hostel (🛏26, €21-22/45/50 🧺): ♿ W D 📶, Sangüesa 2, ☎648289403 📱, bike rental

H Alda Centro (€80/85): 📶, Plaza Virgen de la O 7, ☎948222270 📱

H Pensión Escaray (€25/50): 📶, Nueva 24, ☎948227825

H Casa Otano (€78): San Nicolás 5, ☎948227036

H Hostal Arriazu (€73-81): Comedias 14, ☎948210202 📱

H Sercotel Europa (€85-130): 🍴 W 📶, Espoz y Mina 11, ☎948221800 📱

H Pensión Mayte (€43/51): W 📶, Av Pio XII 32, ☎686479966 📱

4

PAMPLONA TO PUENTE LA REINA

24.1km (15.0mi), ▲ 434M / ▼ 538M, ⏱ 6-7 Hours
P 37%, 8.9km, U 63%, 15.2km, **Difficulty:** ▬▬□

💡 Leave Pamplona by way of the Citadel park and climb to the small town of Cizur Menor. The steep climb to Alto de Perdón affords wonderful views, but be careful on the loose, rocky descent. A worthwhile detour leads to the enigmatic church of Eunate. Be prepared for less shade today as you enter a more temperate climate with fields of wheat and grapes.

5.2 Cizur Menor A 🍴🛒➕🚌

A Orden de Malta (asoc, 🛏27, €7): 📶, ☎616651330, 🕐May-Sept, run by the Sanjuanista Order of Malta with the feel of a parochial albergue

11.4 Zariquiegui A 🍴

A San Andrés (🛏26, €15): 🍴📶📶📶📶, Camino de Santiago 4, ☎626161183 📝

17.2 Uterga A H 🍴

A H Camino del Perdón (🛏16, €14/-/65): 🍴📶📶📶, Mayor 61, ☎948344598 📝
A H Casa Baztán (🛏26, €14/-/60): 🍴📶📶📶📶, Mayor 46, ☎948344528 📝

21.8 Óbanos H 🍴🛒➕☕🚌

1. **H Mamerto** (€35/50): 📶📶, San Lorenzo 7, ☎948344344 📝
2. **H Casa Rural Raichu** (€54-63/60-70): 📶📶📶, ☎948344285, Larrotagaña 2 📝
3. **H Studio Villazón** (studio apt €72/80): 📶📶📶, San Sebastián 5, ☎620441467 📝

24.1 Puente la Reina A H 🍴🛒➕☕ℹ️⛺🚌

1. **A Padres Reparadores** (par, 🛏96, €10): 📶📶📶📶, Crucifijo 1, ☎948340050, 🕐12pm all year, nice green yard/garden, has credenciales
2. **A H Jakue** (🛏46, €20-25/-/48-55): 🍴📶📶📶📶📶, Irunbidea 34, ☎948341017 📝, 🕐12pm Mar 15-Oct, located in hotel
3. **A H El Puente** (🛏36, €16/-/43): 🍴📶📶📶📶, Fueros 57, ☎661705642 📝, 🕐Apr-Oct
4. **A H Estrella Guía** (🛏6, €20/-/56-60 🍳): 🍴📶📶📶, Población 2, ☎622262431 📝,
5. **A H Santiago Apostól** (🛏100, €13/25/35): 📶📶📶, ☎948340220 📝, 🕐11am Apr-Oct, ⛺**Camping El Real** at same establishment
6. **H El Cerco** (€57/89): 🍴📶, Rodrigo Ximenez de Rada 36, ☎948341269 📝

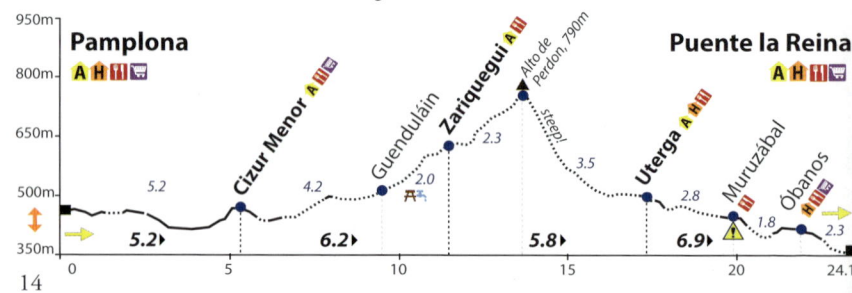

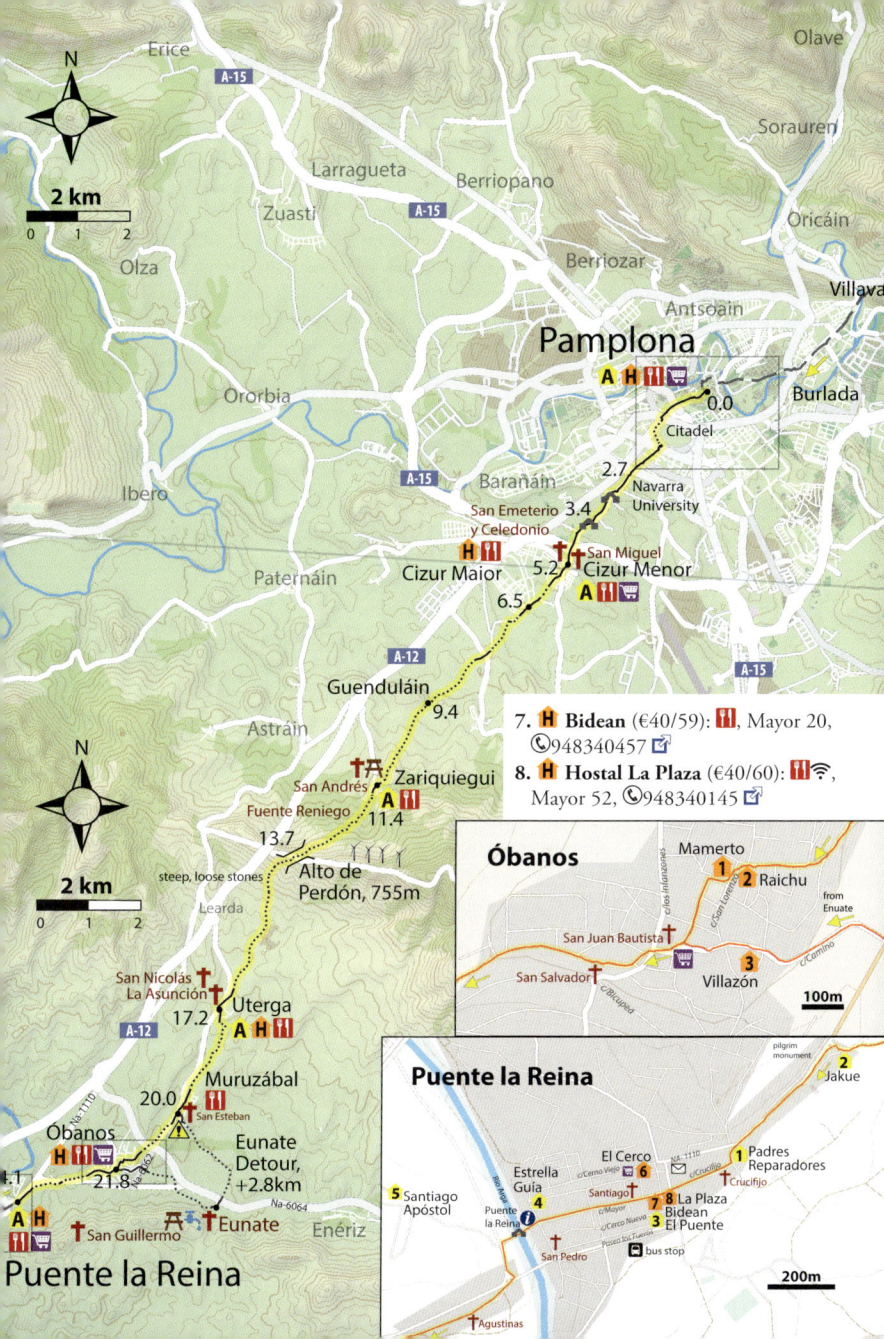

5

PUENTE LA REINA TO ESTELLA

22.0km (13.7mi), ▲ 402M / ▼ 331M, ⏱ 5-6 HOURS
🅿 28%, 6.2km, 🆄 72%, 15.8km, DIFFICULTY: 🟥🟧⬜

☀ A stage primarily on dirt paths with gently rolling ups and downs, which passes through picturesque medieval towns. Authentic stretches of Roman road and a Roman bridge invite walkers to step back in time. Be prepared for little shade and some road noise from A-12 highway around Lorca. A day of beautiful scenery with fields and vineyards. A more remote alternate route via Luquín splits before Villatuerta or can be joined from Irache in the following stage.

5.2 Mañeru 🅰🅷🍴🛒➕☕🚌

🅰🅷 **El Cantero** (🛏26, €14/45/55): 🔑📶⊙, Esperanza 2, ☎948342142 📝, 📅May-Oct

7.8 Cirauqui 🅰🅷🍴🛒➕☕🚌

🅰🅷 **Maralotx** (🛏32, €16-20/60/76): 🍴🆆🅳📶⊙, San Román 30, ☎678635208 📝, 📅Mar-Oct

13.5 Lorca 🅰🅷🍴🛒🚌

🅰🅷 **La Bodega del Camino** (🛏36, €15/38/45): 🍴🔑🆆🅳📶⊙, Placeta 8, ☎948541162 📝, 📅May-Oct, groups all year

🅰🅷 **De Lorca** (🛏14, €14/-/32): 🔑🆆📶, Mayor 40, ☎948541190, 📅Apr-Oct

🅷 **Casa Nahia** (€72/84): 🔑🆆🅳📶⊙ (garage with tools), Ctra Pamplona 9, ☎660444640 📝

18.0 Villatuerta 🅰🅷🍴🛒➕☕🚌

1. 🅰🅷 **La Casa Mágica** (🛏37, €18/-/70): 🍴🔑🆆🅳🅱📶, Rebote 5, ☎602259283 📝, restored historical building, no bunk beds, yoga and meditation offered
2. 🅰🅷 **Etxeurdina** (🛏14, €18/-/55 🌙): 🔑📶⊙, Río Iranzu 3, ☎621267282 📝
3. 🅷 **643 km** (€50-55): 🔑📶, Plaza Rebote 3, ☎615003690 📝

Estella city map and accommodations on p.18-19.

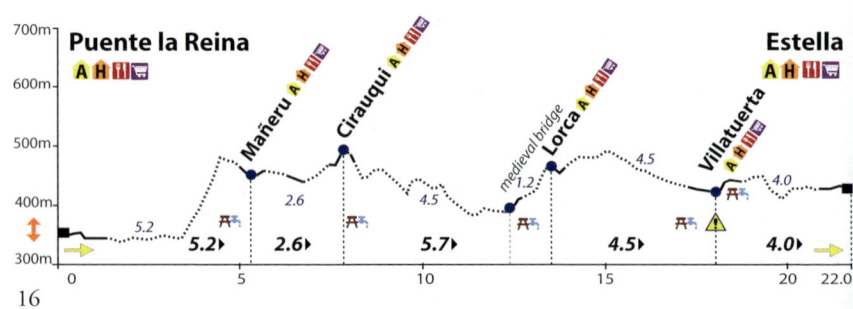

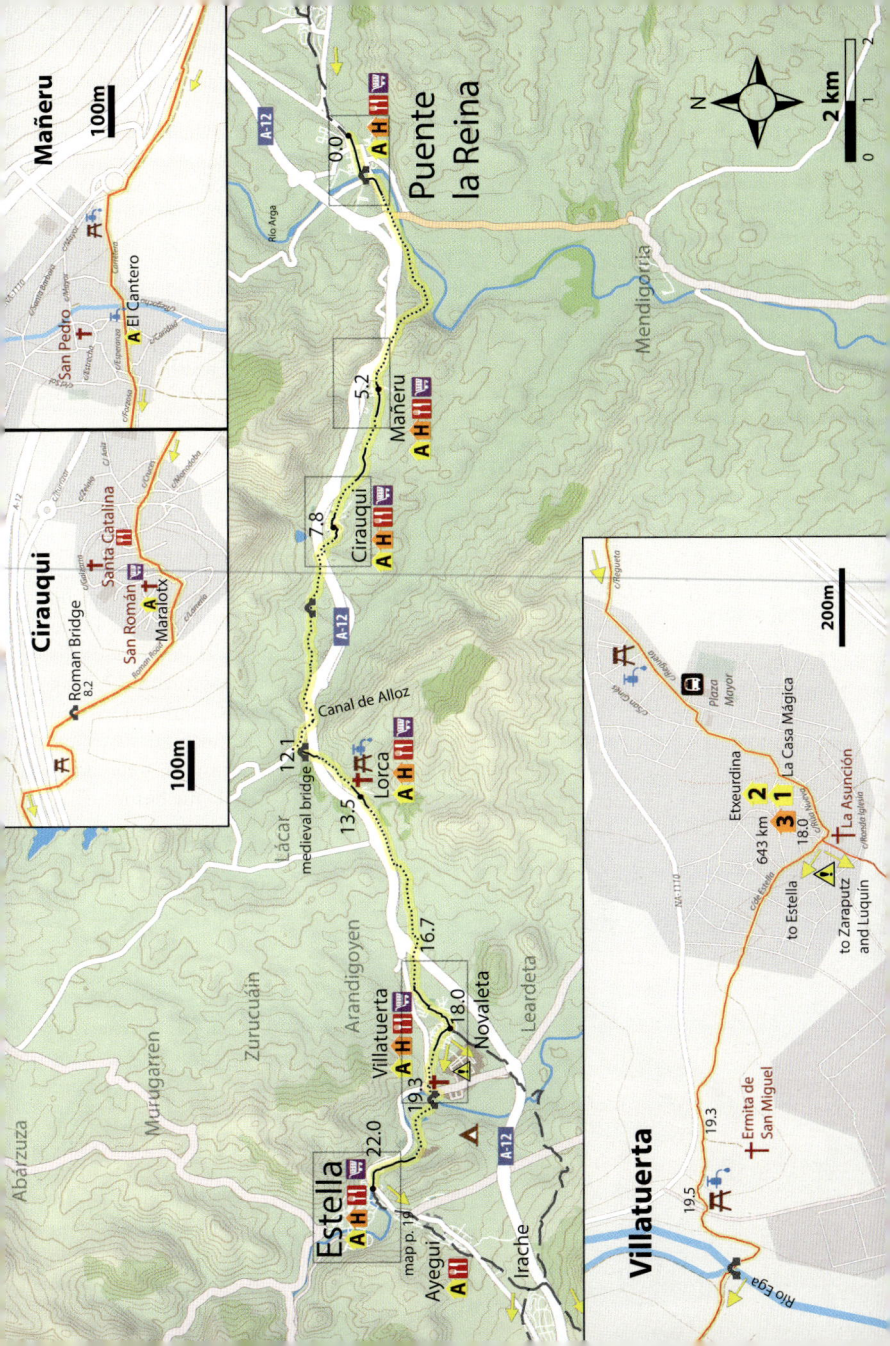

CAMINO DE SANTIAGO: CAMINO FRANCÉS

22.0 Estella 🅰🅷🍴🛒⊙⊕❿ℹ▲🚉 Pop. 14,251 📖 Basque *Lizarra*: "old church" 📖 Latin *stellae*: "s

1. **🅰 Municipal** (⊟96, €8): 🅺🆆🅳🛜, Rúa 50, ☏948550200 📱, ⊙Feb-Nov, crowded
2. **🅰🅷 Hostería de Curtidores** (⊟30, €16-18/-/48-52): 🅺🆆🅳🛜⊙, Curtidores 43, ☏948550070 📱
3. **🅰 ANFAS** (⊟34, €10): 🅺🆆🅳🛜⊙, Cordeleros 7, ☏639011688 📱, ⊙12pm May-Sept, employs adults with intellectual disabilities
4. **🅰🅷 Hostal Ágora** (⊟26, €20-22/-/78): 🅺🆆🅳🛜⊙, Callizo Pelaires 3, ☏948546574 📱, ⊙Feb-D
5. **🅰 San Miguel** (par, ⊟36, don): 🍴🅼🆆, Mercado Viejo 18, ☏948550431, ⊙12:30pm Apr-Oct
6. **🅰🅷 Alda** (€16/45/58): 🛜, Plaza Santiago 41, ☏948030137 📱
7. **🅰🅷 Capuchinos Rocamador** (par, ⊟54, €15-20/35/45): 🍴🅺🆆🅳🛜, Rocamador 6, ☏948550549, ⊙11am summer, all year, call ahead in winter, adjoined to Capuchin convent
8. **🅷 Hostal Cristina** (€50/75): 🛜, Baja Navarra 1, ☏948550450
9. **🅷 Hospedería Chapitel** (€75/95): 🍴🛜, Chapitel 1, ☏948551090 📱, massage available
10. **🅷 Pensión Buen Camino** (€40/55): 🅺🛜, San Nicolás 27, ☏948550337
11. **🅷 Hostal El Volante** (€45-50/68): 🍴🆆🅳🛜, Merkatondoa 2, ☏948553957 📱
▲🅷🅰 **Camping Lizarra** (dm €12.05, camping €27, bungalow $85+): 🍴🛜🛏, Paraje Ordoiz, ☏948551733 📱, off route

---

"Estella [is] full of good bread and the best wine and meat and fish, and plenty of all good things."

Codex Calixtinus

Houses line the Ega River in Estella

22.0 Estella: Development began under King Sancho Ramírez in the early 11th century after a shooting star led to a Virgin Mary statue in a cave (Basílica del Puy houses the statue). Sancho encouraged French settlement, and the town flourished with vibrant pilgrim business, agriculture, and textile industries of wool and leather. The town grew wealthy, and important religious and civic institutions were built, giving the nickname *Estella la bella* ("Estella the beautiful").

As in Pamplona, ethnic neighborhoods grew up, separating Navarros, Francos, and Jews. By the 14th century, Jews made up 10% of the population. In 1328, much of the Jewish community was massacred in a riot, and the rest were forced to convert in the 15th-century Inquisition. The Black Plague halved the population of Estella in the 14th century.

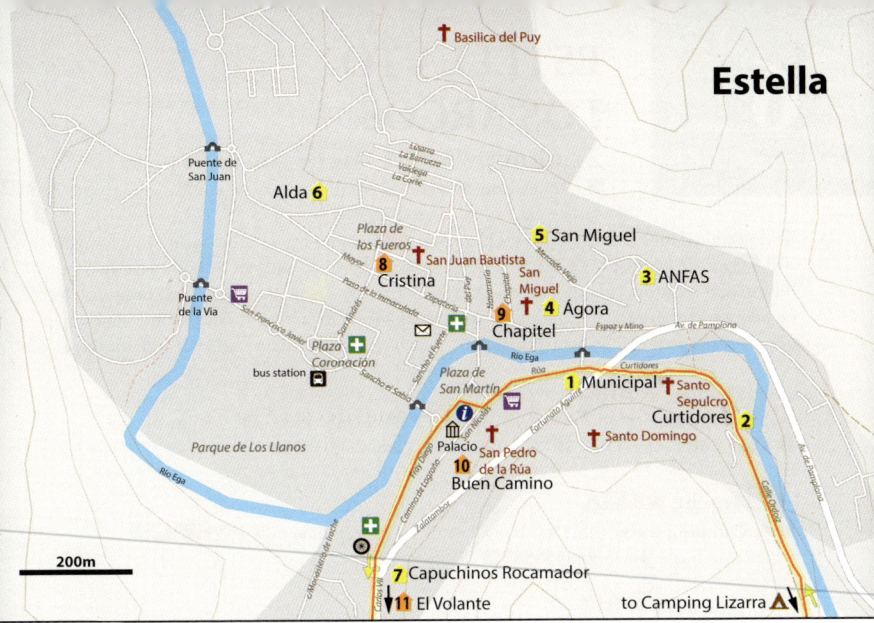

Estella

Historic Churches and Buildings:
- ✝ **Iglesia de Santo Sepulcro**: On the R as you enter town, this façade shows Santiago among the apostles.
- 🏛 **Palacio de los Reyes de Navarra/Museo Gustavo de Maeztu**: (Free, ⓈTu-S 9:30am-1:30pm, 4-7pm high season, Su 11am-4pm) Interesting example of civil Romanesque architecture, note the fine capitals that depict deadly sins and the battle of Roland and Ferragut
- ✝ **Iglesia de San Pedro de la Rúa**: An impressive 12/13th-century fortified church that contains important relics, such as a piece of the true cross and Saint Andrew's shoulder bone.
- ✝ **Iglesia de San Miguel**: A fortress-like 12th-century church with a spectacular north portal.
- ✝ **Iglesia de San Juan Bautista**: Built by Sancho el Fuerte and containing images of Santiago Peregrino.
- ✝ **Basílica del Puy**: Built on the spot that legend holds a Virgin was found in 1085; the wooden silver-covered statue is still on display within.

Estella
Aug: Patron saint San Andrés with running of the bulls
May 25: Virgen del Puy with traditional dances
Thursday is market day.
Suckling pig is a local delicacy (*gorrín asado*).

6

ESTELLA TO LOS ARCOS

21.6km (13.4mi), ▲ 383M / ▼ 361M, ⏱ 5-6 Hours
🅿 19%, 4.1km, U 81%, 17.5km, **Difficulty:** 🟧🟧⬜

💡 Rolling red hills and vineyards lead to a place of Camino legend, the Irache wine fountain. Villamayor de Monjardín provides a welcome halfway stop, with an imposing castle on the hilltop and a historic fountain at the entrance. The last 12km are remote and beautiful, but be prepared for little shade and only a food truck for services. The alternate route via Luquín offers a more remote but demanding path, which rejoins the main trail after Villamayor.

1.6 Ayegui A H 🍴🚌
A San Cipriano (muni, 🛏42, €15): 🍴W D 📶, ☎948554331, ⏱1pm all year
H Casa Luisa (€85-110): 🍴📶, San Lázaro 9, ☎848460100

4.3 Irache H 🍴🛒▲
H ▲ Camping Iratxe (dbl €44, bungalow €75-112, camping €20-25): 🍴🛒🏊, Prado de Irache 14, ☎948555555

7.4 Azqueta A H 🍴
A H La Perla Negra (🛏7, €22/-/55): 🍴W 📶, Carrera 18, ☎627114797

9.2 Villamayor de Monjardín A H 🚌
A H Oasis Trails (asoc, 🛏25, €12/35/40): 🍴📶, Plaza 4, ☎948537136, ⏱Apr-Oct, fireplace, run by Dutch Christian evangelistic association
A H Villamayor de Monjardín (🛏20, €15/-/40): 🅺W D 📶, Mayor 1, ☎677660586, ⏱2pm Mar-Nov

21.6 Los Arcos A H 🍴🛒➕€ℹ🚌, ℹ Plaza Fueros, ☎948640077, 📶 at library
1. **A** Isaac Santiago (muni, 🛏70, €8): 🅺, San Lázaro, ☎948441091, ⏱12pm Apr-Oct
2. **A H** La Fuente Casa de Austria (🛏54, €12/-/35): 🅺W D 📶, Estanco 5, ☎948640797, ⏱1pm Feb-Dec 15
3. **A H** ⭐ Casa de la Abuela (🛏32, €15/-/40-50): 🅺W D 📶, Plaza de la Fruta 8, ☎948640250, ⏱12pm Mar-Oct, house of owner's grandmother

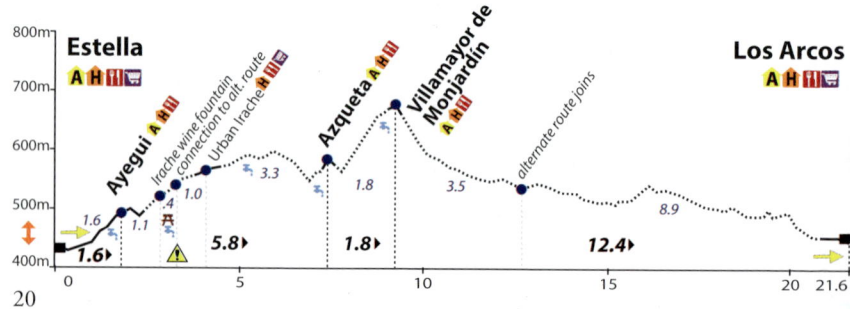

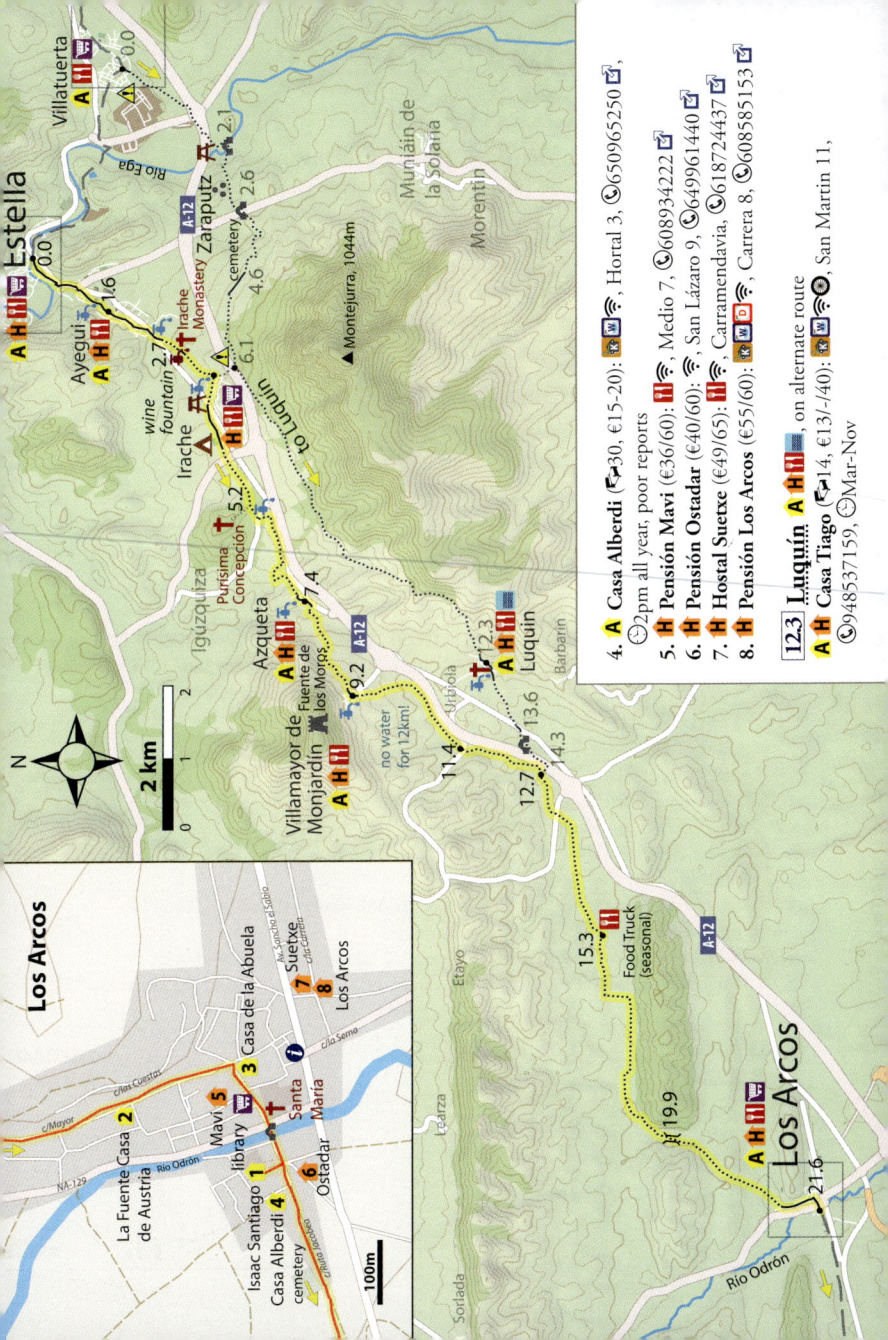

7

LOS ARCOS TO LOGROÑO

27.5km (17.1mi), ▲ 410M / ▼ 480M, ⏱ 7-8 Hours
🅿 37%, 10.2km, 🆄 63%, 17.3km, **Difficulty:** 🟥🟧⬜

💡 Endless fields of golden wheat lead to the hilltop medieval towns of Sansol and Torres del Río. The rolling hills to Viana have a remote feel with little shade and no services. From Viana to Logroño, the trail passes through a birdwatching area and enters into the autonomous region of La Rioja, best known for its superlative red wine.

6.8 Sansol A H 🍴 🛒 ➕ 🅿

- **A Sansol** (🛏26, €15): 🍴 W D 📶, Barrio Nuevo 4, ☎948648473, 📅Mar-Oct
- **A Palacio de Sansol** (🛏32, €16-18/62/77): 🍴 K W D O, Sindicato 1, ☎646334730 📧, 📅Apr-Oct
- **A Karma** (🛏12, €10): W D 📶 O, Taconera 11, ☎665170116
- **H El Olivo** (€25/40-50 🛏): K W D 📶, Taconera 9, ☎948648345 📧

7.7 Torres del Río A H 🍴 🛒 ➕ ℹ 🅿

1. **A Casa Mariela** (🛏50, €13-15): K W O, Valeriano Ordóñez 6, ☎948648251, 📅10am all year
2. **A H La Pata de Oca** (🛏32, €15/-/60): 🍴 W D 📶 🚻, Mayor 5, ☎948378457 📧, 📅a. y.
3. **A H San Andrés** (€15/60/75): 🍴 W D 📶 🚻, Jesús Ordoñez 6, ☎948648472 📧

18.4 Viana A H 🍴 🛒 ➕ ℹ 🅿

1. **A Andrés Muñoz** (muni, 🛏54 in triple bunks, €8): K W D, Ruinas de San Pedro, ☎948645530, 📅Mar 15-Oct, call in winter
2. **⚠ A Parroquial de Viana** (par, 🛏15 mats, don): 🍴, Plaza de los Fueros, ☎948645037, **Temporarily closed**
3. **A H Izar** (🛏44, €15/-/40 🛏): K W D 📶 O, El Cristo 6, ☎660071349 📧, 📅12pm Mar-Nov
4. **H Palacio de Pujadas** (€75-115): 🍴, Navarro Villoslada 30, ☎948646464 📧, historic building in Old City
5. **H Casa Armendáriz** (€30/50): 🍴, Navarro Villoslada 19, ☎948645078 📧
6. **H Pensión San Pedro** (€40/50): 📶, Medio San Pedro 13, ☎948645927 📧

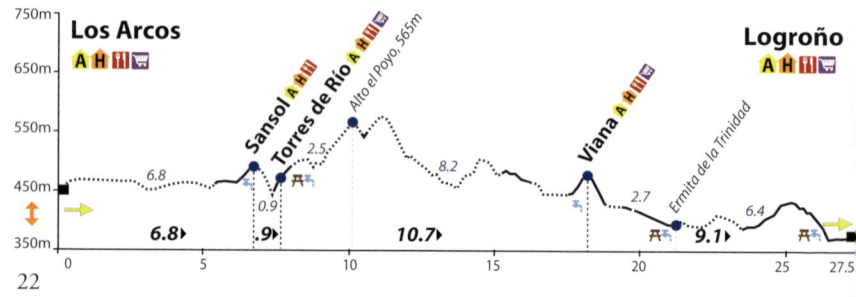

CAMINO DE SANTIAGO: CAMINO FRANCÉS

27.5 **Logroño** is the capital of the winemaking region of La Rioja. With its strategic location on the banks of the Río Ebro and right along the border between Aragón, Navarra, and Castile y León, it's no wonder why Logroño was a much fought-over commodity. Constant warfare may be a reason that practically nothing remains of the many medieval pilgrim hospitals. Logroño is mentioned in pilgrim records as a place where a duty of two *reales* was collected.

The main churches to visit are **Iglesia de Santa María la Redonda** ("Saint Mary the Round"), with Baroque façade and stork-topped spires. **Iglesia de San Bartolomé** was built in the 13th century, and Iglesia de Santiago del Real boasts an impressive 17th-century Santiago Matamoros above the entrance and numerous Santiago images within. On the sidewalk just before Iglesia de Santiago, there is a large game called *Juego de Oca,* which is similar to Chutes and Ladders.

Calle Laurel is the nightlife zone with over 60 bars and restaurants, locally known as "*la senda de los elefantes*" (the elephant walk), since sampling wine in too many establishments may have you walking out on all fours. The town of Clavijo, where the mythical Battle of Clavijo took place, is located about 16km from Logroño and makes an interesting side trip by bus.

☼ Just before the Puente de Piedra bridge entering Logroño, on the left is a **pilgrim information office**, ☏941275982

⚜ **Logroño**
Sept: Fiesta de San Mateo, a wine festival featuring grape crushing exhibitions

Santiago Matamoros at Iglesia de Santiago in Logroño

75 Logroño A H 🍴🛒🛍️🔧➕⚕️ℹ️⛺🏦🚉✈️ Pop. 152,641, 🏛 Celtic-Latin, *ilo Gronnio*: "ford/pass"
A Municipal (⛺68, €10): 🍳 W D 📶, Ruavieja 32, ☎941248686, 🕐Mar-Oct, crowded & stuffy, courtyard with foot pool
A H Santiago Apóstol (⛺78, €12/-/48-65): 🍴K W D 📶, Ruavieja 42, ☎941256976, 🕐all year
A H Logroño Centro: (⛺18, €18/68/71): 🍳 📶⚙, Marqués de San Nicolás 31, ☎678495109 📧
A H Winederful Hostel (⛺30, €21-/60): Herrerias 2-14, ☎941139618 📧
A Iglesia de Santiago (par, ⛺30, don): 🍴, Barriocepo 6, ☎941209501, 🕐all year, communal meals
A H Logroño la Balbaína (⛺30, €15/40/53): 🍳 W D 📶, Capitán Gallarza 10, ☎941254226 📧
A H Albas (⛺22, €15-17/-/48): 🍳 W D 📶⚙, Martínez Flamarique 4, ☎941700832 📧, 🕐11am a.y.
H Sercotel Portales (€100-120): 📶, Portales 85, ☎941502794 📧
H Hotel Murrieta (€77/82): 🍴📶, Marqués de Murrieta 1, ☎941224150 📧
H Hotel Condes de Haro (€75): 🍴📶, Saturnino Ulargui 6, ☎941208500 📧
H Pensión Logroño (€45/50): 📶, Canalejas 7, ☎941101186
H Hostal Numantina (€53/71): Sagasta 4, ☎941251411 📧
H Pensión La Rioja (€38-43/43-63): 📶, ☎638552126, Diego de Velázquez 8 📧
H Camping La Playa (dbl bungalow €66, tent €14): Playa 6, ☎941252253 📧, +850m

8

LOGROÑO TO NÁJERA

29.8km (18.5mi), ▲ 429M / ▼ 320M, ⊕ 7-9 Hours
P 38%, 11.3km, U 62%, 18.5km, **Difficulty:** ▬▬▬

💡 A rolling stage with a mix of natural walking paths and sections on or close to roads. After Logroño, there is a pleasant stretch through a green park with a reservoir lake. The path is close to the highway between Navarrete and Ventosa, and the approach to Nájera is decidedly industrial, but before Nájera some classic Rioja red earth vineyards can be seen.

12.8 Navarrete
c/Cuesta Caño ☎941441062 in summer
1. **A** Municipal (🛏50, €10): San Juan, ☎941440722, ⊕1pm Mar-Oct
2. **A H** Camino de las Estrellas (🛏40, €15/-/50): Burgos 9, ☎618051392, ⊕all year, bike storage and workshop
3. **A** La Casa del Peregrino (🛏20, €15): Huertas 3, ☎630982928
4. **A H** Buen Camino (🛏10, €15/31/40): La Cruz 2, ☎681252222
5. **A** La Iglesia (🛏15, €15/-/48): Mayor Alta 2, ☎602265787
6. **A H** El Cántaro (🛏22, €15/28-45/35-50): Herrerías 16, ☎941441180
7. **H** Villa de Navarrete (€35-48/45-50): La Cruz 2C, ☎941440318
8. **H** Rey Sancho (€70-85): Mayor Alta 5, ☎941441378
9. **H** Casa Peregrinando (€58/66): Mayor Alta 34, ☎941441324
10. **H** A la Sombra del Laurel (€35/50): Burgos 52, ☎639861110, ⊕all year

19.6 Ventosa
A San Saturnino (🛏42, €14): Mayor 33, ☎941441899, ⊕1pm all year, fireplace, shop with basic food
H Las Águedas (€85-89): Plaza de Santa Coloma 11, ☎941441774

29.8 Nájera
1. **A** Municipal (🛏48, €6): ☎941360041, ⊕all year, 1pm summer
2. **A** El Peregrino Najerino (🛏28, €11): San Fernando 90, ☎613251499
3. **A H** Puerta de Nájera (🛏32, €15-20/-/40-45): Ribera del Najerilla 1, ☎941362317, ⊕Mar-Oct
4. **A H** Nido de Cigüeña (🛏20, €15/-/35): San Miguel 4, ☎941896027
5. **A H** Sancho III - La Judería (🛏16, €12/20/30): S. Marcial 5, ☎941-361138

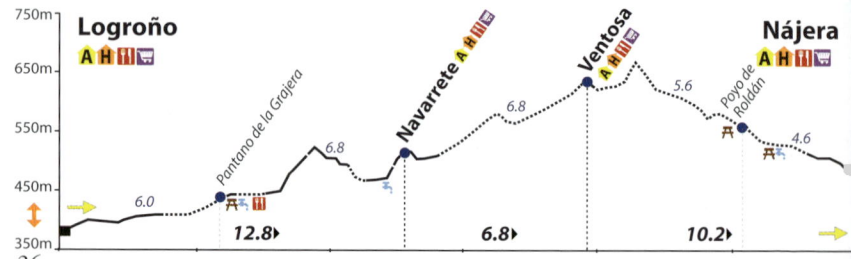

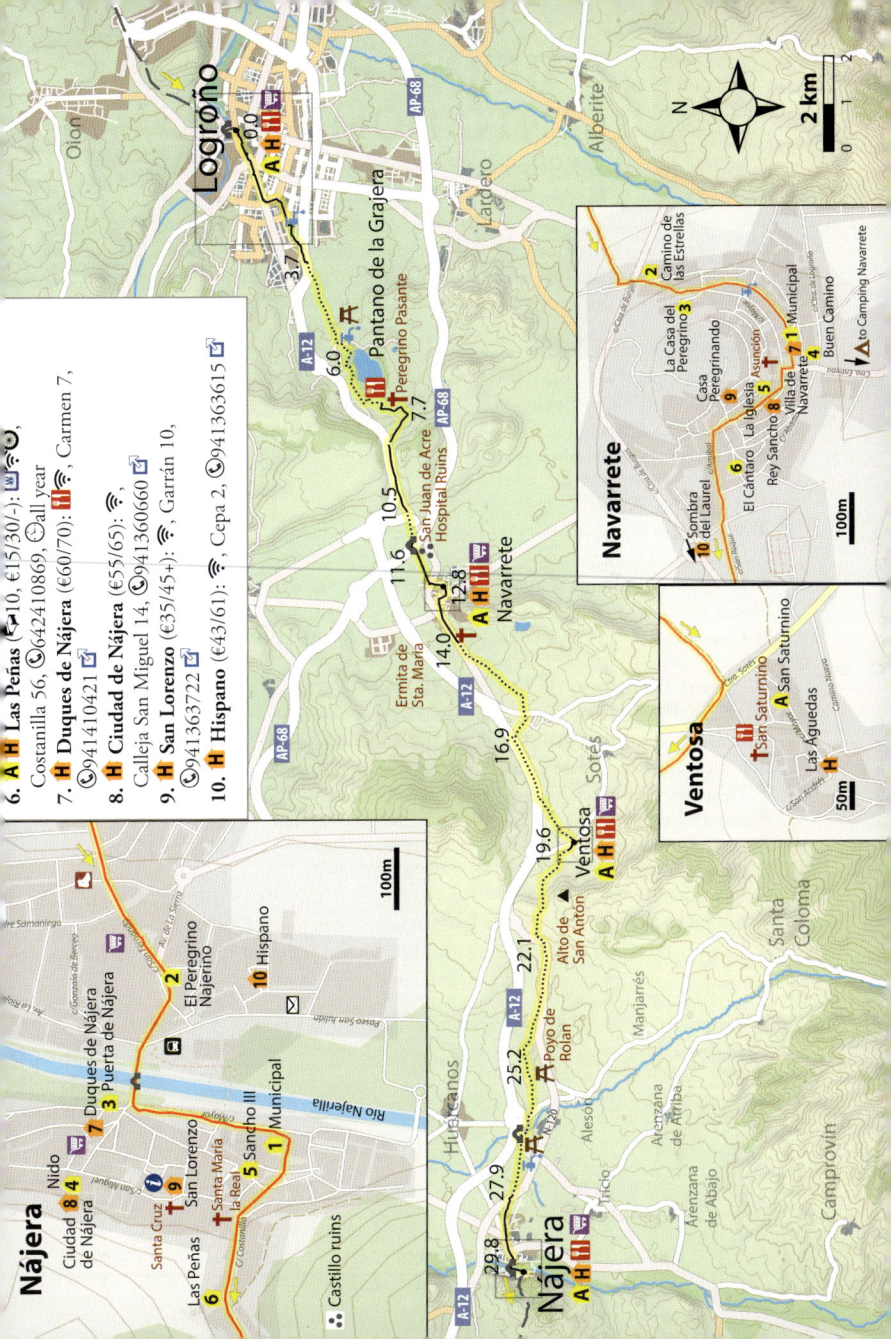

9

NÁJERA TO SANTO DOMINGO

20.9km (13.0mi), ▲ 377M / ▼ 225M, ⏱ 5-6 Hours
P 33%, 6.9km, **U** 67%, 14.0km, **Difficulty:** ▬▭▭

💡 Much of this day is on wide farm tracks through fields of grain and grapes, far from the busy highway. Prepare for little shade and few places to get water on this more remote day with fewer services. A golf course and ghost town in Cirueña feel strangely out of place.

5.8 Azofra A H 🍴 🛒 ✚ 🚌
1. **A** ⭐ **Municipal** (⛺60, €15): 🛏 W D ◎, Parras 7, ☎941379049, ⏱ all year, 2 beds/room, foot pool
2. **H** **Pensión La Plaza** (€40/55): 🍴 🛜, Plaza de España 7, ☎629828702 🗒
3. **H** **Real Casona de las Amas** (€179+): W 🛜, Mayor 5, ☎941416103 🗒, spa, luxurious

15.0 Cirueña A H 🍴
1. **A** **Virgen de Guadalupe** (⛺35, €15): 🍴 W D 🛜, Barrio Alto 1, ☎638924069 🗒, ⏱ Mar 15-Oct 15
2. **A H** **Victoria** (⛺12, €15/30/46): 🍴 🛏 W D 🛜, San Andrés 10, ☎941426105 🗒, ⏱ Mar-Oct
3. **H** **Casa Victoria** (€34/48): 🛏 W D 🛜 ◎, Plaza del Horno 8, ☎941426105 🗒

20.9 Santo Domingo de la Calzada
A H 🍴 🛒 ✚ € 🛈 ▲ 🚌 🗒 "Saint Dominic of the Causeway" after the town's founder
1. **A** **Cofradía del Santo** (asoc, ⛺184, €13): 🛏 🛜 ◎, Mayor 38, ☎941343390 🗒, ⏱ 11:30am all year, modern facilities, laundromat next door, chickens!
2. **H** **Hospedería Cisterciense** (€40/60): Pinar 2, ☎941340700 🗒
3. **H** **Rey Pedro I** (€60-75): 🛜, San Roque 9, ☎941341160 🗒
4. **H** **El Molino de Floren** (€63-78/77-83): 🍴 🛜, Margubete 5, ☎941342931 🗒
5. **H** **Parador** (€120-200): 🍴 🛜, Santo 3, ☎941340300 🗒, historic pilgrim hospice
6. **H** **La Catedral** (€35-61/48-66): 🛜, Isidoro Salas 49, ☎651948260 🗒
7. **H** **RoomConcept** (€32-55/44-65): W 🛜, Alberto Etchegoyen 2, ☎941342366 🗒
8. **H** **Parador Bernardo de Fresneda** (€74-100): 🛜, San Francisco 1, ☎941341150 🗒

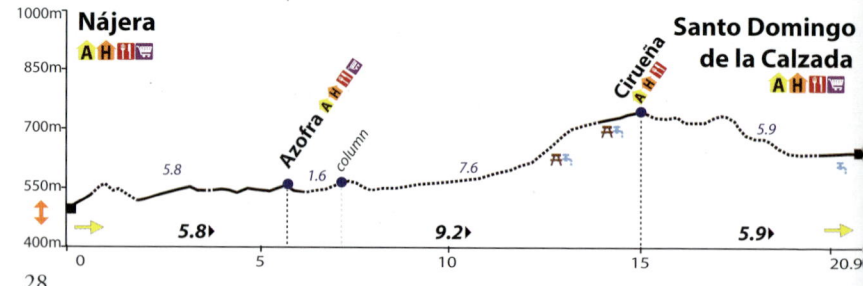

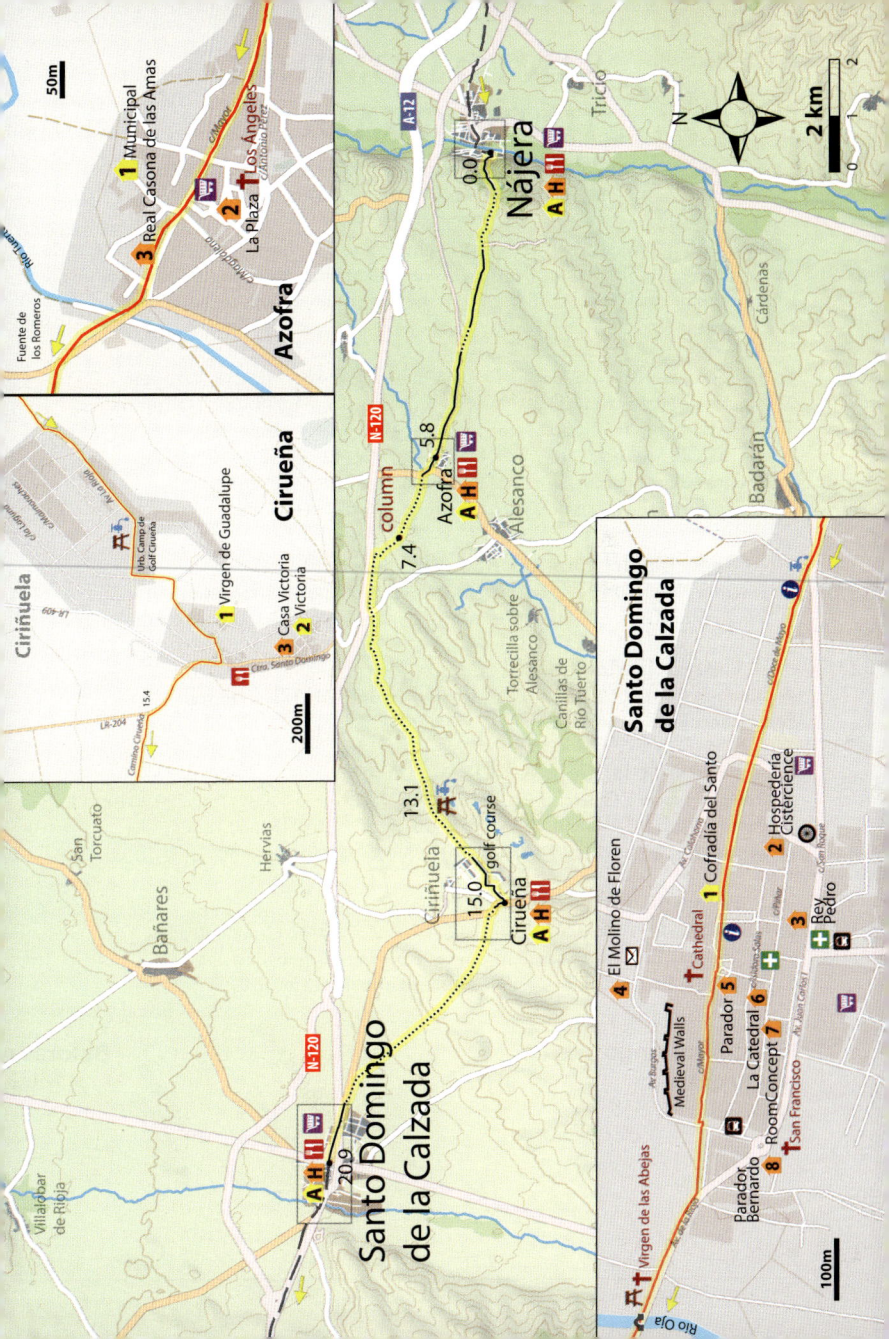

10 SANTO DOMINGO TO BELORADO

22.3km (13.9mi), ▲ 357M / ▼ 225M, ⏱ 5-6 Hours
P 28%, 6.2km, U 72%, 16.1km, **Difficulty:** ▰▰▱▱

About half of this day consists of paths right next to busy highway N-120. Luckily, there are frequent small villages that offer some respite and services. Vast cornfields characterize the landscape as the trail enters Castilla y León, the largest autonomous region of Spain.

6.6 Grañon
1. **A** ★ San Juan Bautista (par, ⛺40 mats, don): ☎941420818, ⊙all year
2. **A** Casa de las Sonrisas (⛺20, don): Mayor 16, ☎687877891, ⊙1pm all year
3. **H** Casa Jacobea (€50/65): Mayor 34, ☎941420684
4. **H** Cerro de Mirabel (€50): Mayor 40, ☎941420798
5. **H** Casa Grande (€150+): El Caño 13, ☎941457726
6. **H** El Cuartel (€44/45): La Hermita 3, ☎627341907

10.3 Redecilla del Camino
A Essentia (⛺10, €14): Mayor 34, ☎606046298, ⊙all year
A San Lázaro (⛺46, €7): Mayor 24, ☎947580283, ⊙a.y., communal meals

12.2 Castildelgado
A Bideluze (⛺16, €15): Mayor 8, ☎616647115, ⊙all year
H El Chocolatero (€60): ☎947588063, along noisy N-120 highway

14.1 Viloria de la Rioja
A Refugio Acacio y Orietta (⛺10, €15): Nuevo 6, ☎947585220, ⊙Apr-Oct
A Parada Viloria (⛺16, €9): Bajera 37, ☎639451660, ⊙Mar-Oct
H MiHotelito (€70-90): Pl Mayor 16, ☎676390240

22.3 Belorado ☎947580815
1. **A H** A Santiago (⛺98, €12-16/35/45): Camino Redoña, ☎677811847, ⊙all year, call in winter, located just before town
2. **A** Refugio Parroquial (⛺24, don): Barrio de El Corro, ☎947580085, ⊙May-Oct, run by volunteers

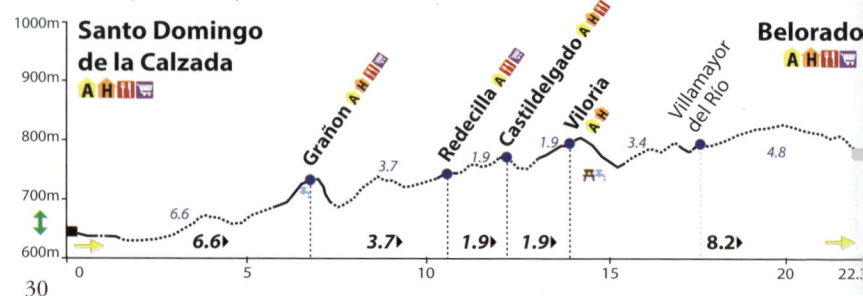

11

BELORADO TO AGÉS

27.5km (17.1mi), ▲ 473M / ▼ 282M, ⏱ 7-8 Hours
🅿 10%, 2.8km, 🅄 90%, 24.8km, **Difficulty:** ▬▬▬

☀ This is a lovely day mostly on earthen paths and passing through frequent villages. The trail crosses through the remote Oca hills, infamous in medieval times as a dangerous route rife with thieves and ne'er-do-wells. Legend credits San Juan de Ortega, disciple of Santo Domingo, with cleaving this path through the thick oak and pine forest with its dense undergrowth. Be extra careful with traffic in Villafranca, where trucks barrel through at full speed.

4.9 Tosantos A 🍴
- **A** ⭐ **San Francisco de Asis** (par, 🛏30, don): 🍴 k, Santa Marina, ☏947580371, 🕒Mar-Oct, communal meals, prayer service with ritual of reading notes by past pilgrims
- **A Los Arancones** (🛏16, €15): 🍴 W D 🛜, La Iglesia, ☏693299063, 🕒all year

6.8 Villambistia A H 🍴
- **A San Roque** (muni, 🛏14, €12 🍳): W D 🛜, Plaza Mayor 1, ☏680501887, 🕒all year
- **H Casa de los Deseos** (€39/59): 🍴 W 🛜, Las Eras 16, ☏947108588

8.4 Espinosa del Camino A 🍴
- **A La Taberna** (🛏22, €12): 🍴 🍳 W D, Barruela 17, ☏618568845
- **A La Campaña** (🛏10, €17 🍳 and dinner): ☏678479361, 🕒15 Jan-15 Dec
- **A Casa las Almas** (🛏12, €12): 🍴 k W D 🛜 ⊙, Barruelo 23, ☏618568845 ✉, camping ok

11.7 Villafranca Montes de Oca A H 🛒 🚌
1. **A H San Antón Abad** (🛏26, €15/40-68/50-83): 🍴 🍳 W D 🛜 ⊙, Hospital 4, ☏947582150 ✉, 🕒Mar-Nov 15, restored historic pilgrim hospital
2. **H La Alpargatería** (€40-45): 🍴 k W 🛜, Mayor 2, ☏686040884
3. **H Pensión Jomer** (€30/45): k W 🛜, Mayor 52, ☏947582146

23.8 San Juan de Ortega A H 🍴 📖 Spanish: "St. John of the nettles"
1. **A Monastery** (par, 🛏70, €15): 🍴 W 🛜, ☏947560438 ✉, 🕒Mar-Oct, poor reports
2. **A El Descanso de San Juan** (🛏6, €15): 🍴 🛜, ☏690398024
3. **H La Henera** (€50/60): 🍴 🛜, La Iglesia 4, ☏606198734 ✉, 🕒Apr-Oct

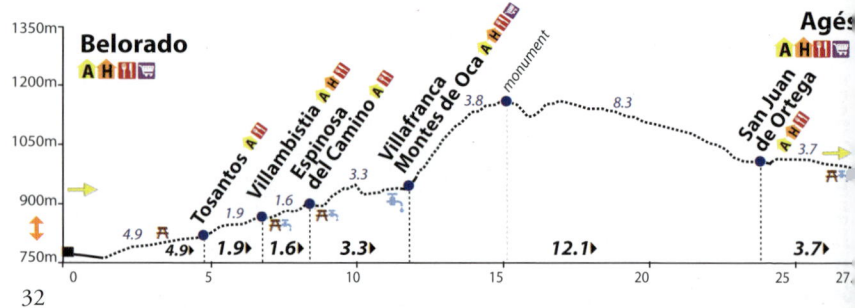

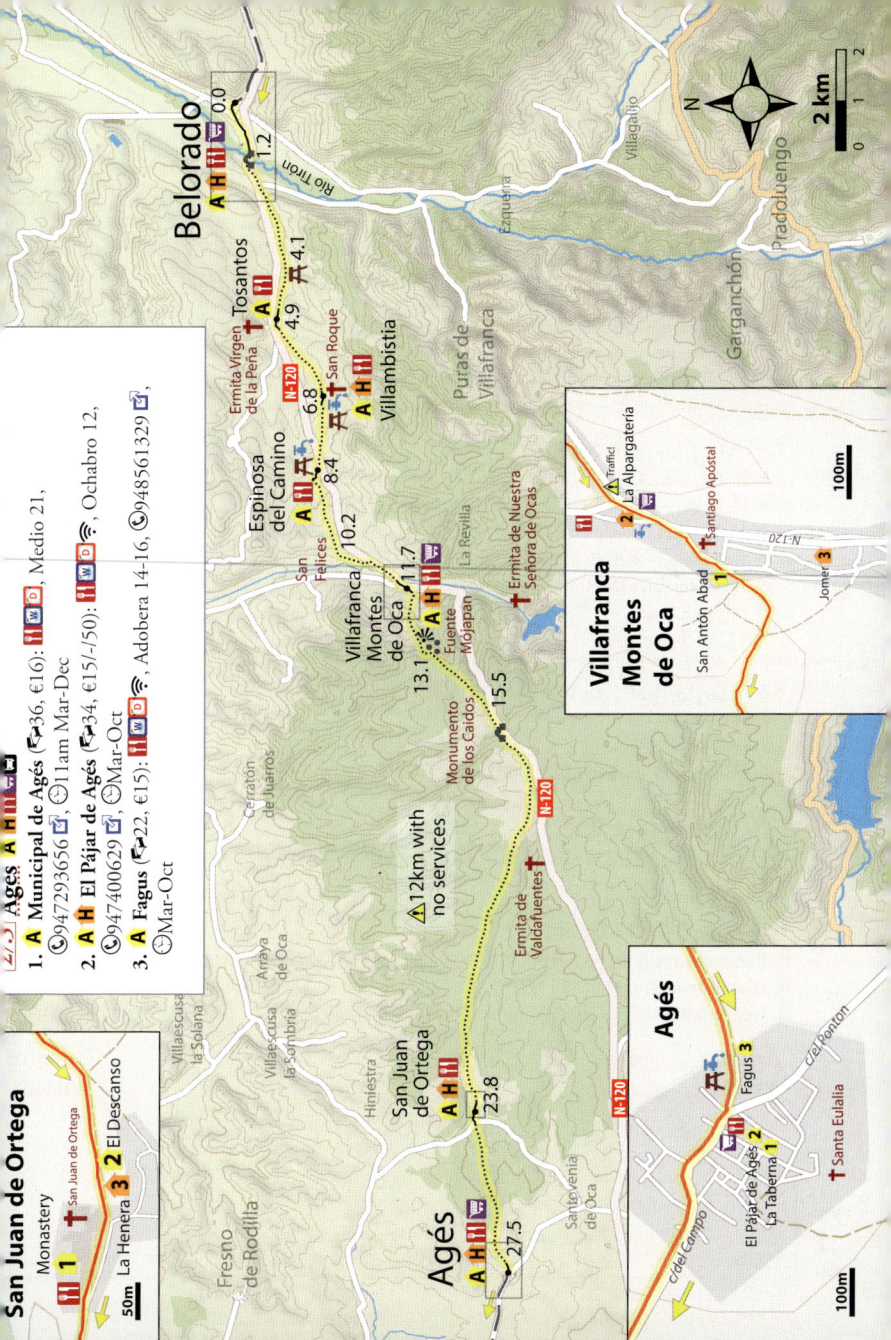

12

AGÉS TO BURGOS

22.4km (13.9mi), ▲ 188M / ▼ 282M, ⏱ 5-6 HOURS
🅿 80%, 17.9km, Ⓤ 20%, 4.5 km, DIFFICULTY: ▬▢▢

💡 The first half of this day consists of quiet roads between quaint villages and peaceful dirt paths through pine forests. Prepare for the second half of the day entering Burgos, which can be a long, tiring walk through urban industrial zones. There are three possible approaches to Burgos; one is not completely marked. We recommend that you take the road less traveled and leave the markings behind at the town of Castañares to cross over the Río Arlanzón and walk along the river on peaceful shady dirt paths. Despite being unmarked, it's easy to navigate as the route follows the river. All options follow the same path for the first 11.9km.

2.5 Atapuerca A H 🍴🛒 Spanish: *ata* "to tie," *puerca* "pig," ⏱ Apr-Sep
1. **A H INpulso Atapuerca** (🛏18, €15-18/36/60): 🔹🔹🔹🔹🔹, Revilla 6, ☎650148195
2. **A H El Peregrino** (🛏36, €12/-/40-50): 🔹🔹🔹🔹, Crta 105, ☎661580882, ⏱1pm
3. **A La Plazuela Verde** (🛏10, €15): 🔹🔹🔹, San Polo 41, ☎658647720, ⏱all year
4. **A La Hutte** (🛏18, €12): 🔹🔹, Enmedio 38, ☎947430320, ⏱1pm all year
5. **H Los Nómadas de Atapuerca** (€45/55): 🔹🔹, La Iglesia 16, ☎610564147
6. **H Papasol** (€60/74): 🔹🔹, Enmedio 36, ☎947430320
7. **H El Pesebre** (€45/55): 🔹, Iglesia 16, ☎610564147

8.8 Cardeñuela de Riopico A H 🍴
1. **A H Via Minera** (🛏26, €8-12/35/45): 🔹🔹🔹🔹🔹, Iglesia 1, ☎652941647, ⏱Mar-Oct, rooms with 2, 4 or 6 beds
2. **A H Santa Fe** (🛏14, €12/33/50): 🔹🔹🔹🔹, Los Huertos 2, ☎626352269

10.9 Orbaneja A H 🍴
A El Peregrino (🛏18, €8-10): 🔹🔹🔹, Principal 1, ☎648604577, ⏱all year
H Fortaleza (€60-65): Principal 31, ☎678116570

14.1 Villafría H 🍴🛒💰🏧
H Buenos Aires (€46/58): 🔹🔹, Vitoria 349, km 245, ☎947483740
H Hostal Iruñako (€50/57): 🔹🔹, Ctra N-1, km 245.5, ☎947484126
H Las Vegas (€48/75): 🔹🔹, Vitoria 319, ☎947484453

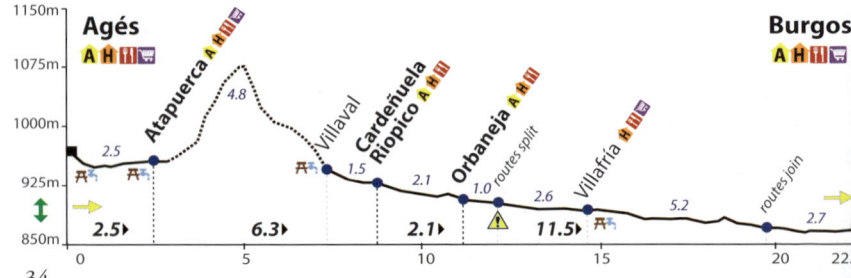

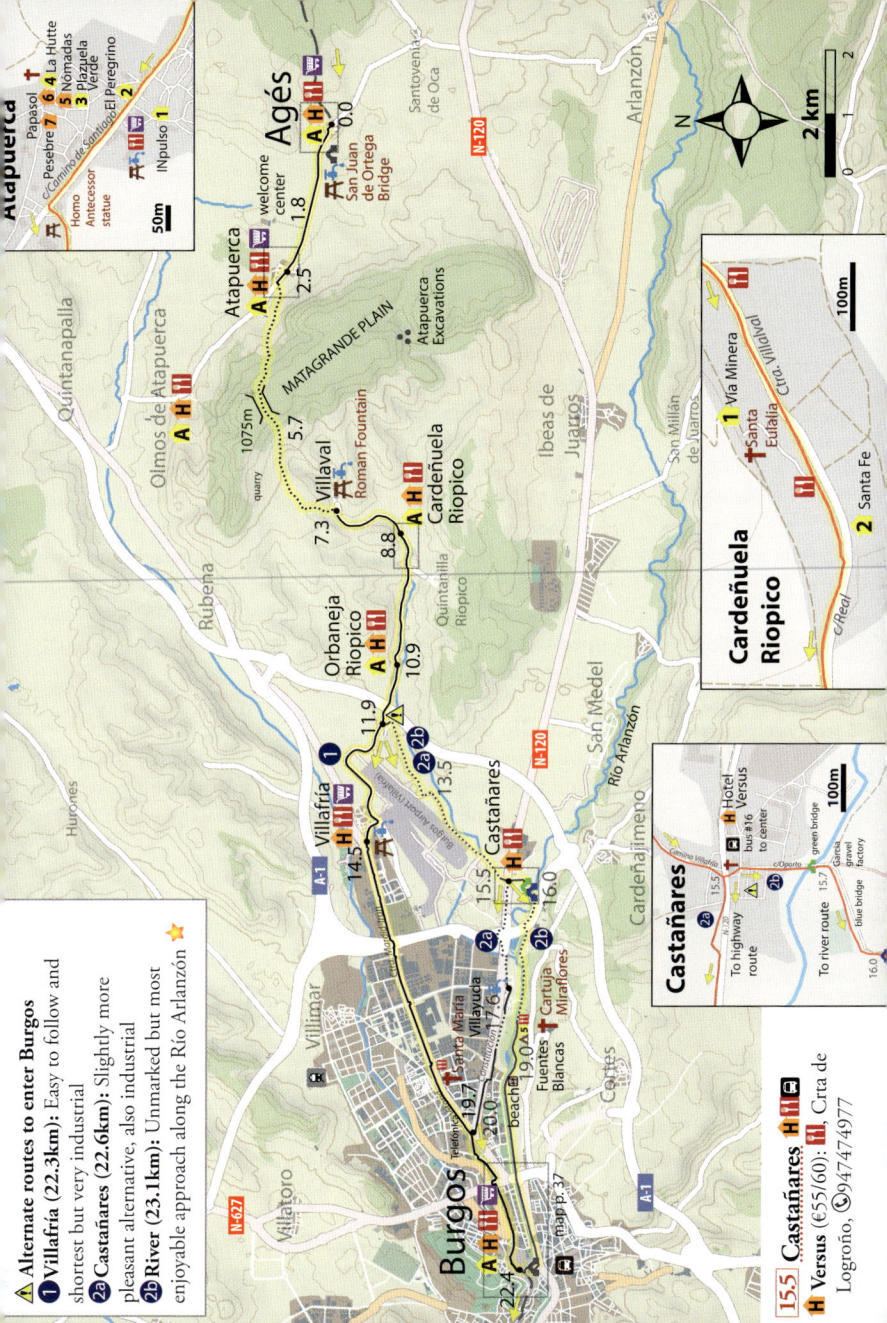

CAMINO DE SANTIAGO: CAMINO FRANCÉS

Burgos
Mar 17: San Antón, including a ceremony of blessing for pets
Spring: La Noche Blanca large cultural event
June: San Pedro y San Pablo festival

Queso de Burgos is a local specialty, a fresh cheese often eaten with honey, quince, or walnuts.

22.3 Burgos is a magnificent city with immeasurable wealth of historic art and architecture. A rest day to visit the sites is well worth your time.

† **Catedral de Burgos:** (€9.50/5 with credential, includes audio guide, variable schedule, most days 10am-7pm), A UNESCO World Heritage site, the entrance fee includes a detailed brochure of the many naves, chapels, and pieces of art. Don't miss the *Capilla del Condestable*, which contains a staggering Mudéjar-Gothic dome, unbelievably realistic 16th-century tombs, the *Retablo de Santa Ana*, created by the famous Gil de Siloé and his son, and the main retablo, also created by Siloé's son. The holiest object for local believers is *Santo Cristo de Burgos*, a sculpture of Jesus on the cross said to be made with real skin and hair (and legend has it, needs to be shaved!) His chapel must be entered from a separate outdoor entrance, as a place of worship as opposed to the rest of the cathedral, which serves more as a museum. Worship areas open 8:30am-1:30pm, 4:30pm-8pm and are to be visited only for prayer (no photos).

Castillo de Burgos (free, 10:30am-5:30pm, open later in summer, 947203857, Cerro de San Miguel) The park around the castle provides a beautiful vantage point over the city; one of the few places you can take in the whole of the cathedral.

Museum of Human Evolution (€6 adults/€4 pilgrims, 10am-8pm, closed Mondays, 902024246, Paseo de la Sierra de Atapuerca) Well-organized museum of the most important artifacts from the Atapuerca excavations. Entrance to the archeological park costs €4-6.

Museo de Burgos (€1, Tu-Sa 10am-2pm, 5-8pm, Su 10am-2pm, 947265875, c/Marianda 13)

Centro de Arte Caja de Burgos
(free modern art museum, 947256550, c/Saldaña)

Arco Santa María (free, M-Sa 11am-2pm, 5-9pm, Su 11am-2pm, 947288868, near Puente de Santa María)

Sacristy ceiling in the Burgos Cathedral

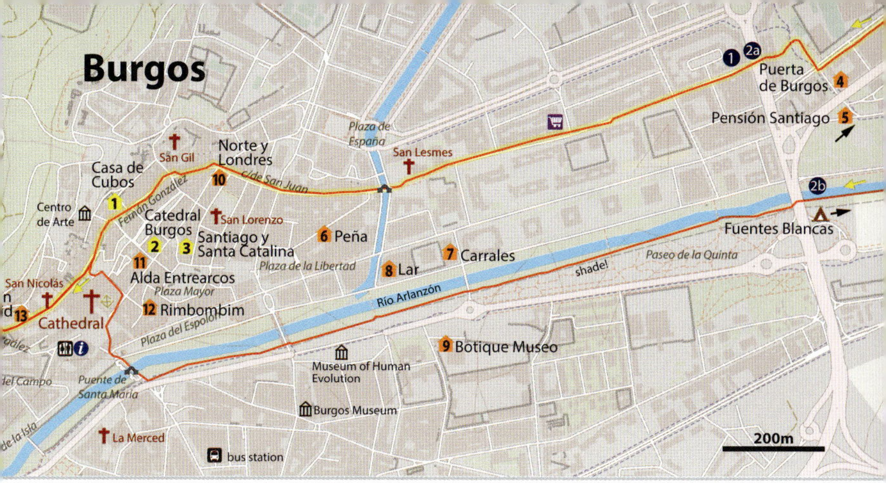

Burgos

22.4 Burgos

1. **A Casa de Cubos** (asoc, ⌂150, €10): Fernán González 28, ☎947460922, ⊙12pm summer, 1pm rest of year, all year, lockers
2. **A H Catedral Burgos** (⌂136, €23-25/60/75): Huerto del Rey 5, ☎623115887
3. **A Santiago y Santa Catalina** (asoc, ⌂16, €11): Lain Calvo 10, ☎947207952
4. **H Puerta de Burgos** (€80-100): Vitoria 69, ☎947241000
5. **H Pensión Santiago** (€44): Santiago Apóstol 8, ☎947046230
6. **H Pensión Peña** (€38): Pueblo 18, ☎947206323
7. **H Happy Hostel Carrales** (€50/81): Puente Gasset 4, ☎947263547
8. **H Hostal Lar** (€50/65): Cardenal Benlloch 1, ☎947209655
9. **H Hotel Boutique Museo Burgos** (€55/65): Ramón y Cajal 10, ☎947257360
10. **H Norte y Londres** (€65-80): Plaza Alonso Martínez 10, ☎947264125
11. **H Alda Entrearcos** (€55/65): Paloma 4, ☎947090630
12. **H Rimbombim** (€71-100): Sombrerería 6, ☎947261200
13. **H Mesón del Cid** (€130-200): Plaza Santa María 8, ☎947208715, cathedral views

pilgrim never goes without sleep   Display in the Museum of Human Evolution

13

BURGOS TO HONTANAS

31.3km (19.4mi), ▲ 316M / ▼ 317M, ⏱ 7-9 Hours
P 24%, 7.5km, U 76%, 23.8km, **Difficulty:** ▬▬▭

💡 This day leaves behind the city pace of Burgos with its whizzing cars and factories, and enters the peaceful and (at times) monotonous landscape of the Meseta, characterized by long flat sections of wheat fields, with nothing but more fields for as far as the eye can see. This is a long stage but has enough intermediary stops with good services to take a few relaxing breaks. Be prepared for little to no shade.

11.2 Tardajos A H 🍴🛒✚€🚌
1. **A Municipal** (🛏18, don): Asunción, 📞947451189, 📅Mar 19-Nov 1, simple and clean
2. **A H La Fábrica** (🛏14, €13/42/50): 🍴 W 📶 ⊚, Fábrica 27, 📞620111939 💻
3. **A H Casa de Beli** (🛏26, €12/50/55): 🍴 W D 📶 ⊚, General Yagüe 16, 📞947451234 💻

13.0 Rabé de las Calzadas A H 🚌
4. **A Liberanos Domine** (🛏24, €12): 🍴 W D 📶, Francisco Ribera 10, 📞695116901 💻
5. **H La Fuente de Rabé** (€47/57): 🍴 W D 📶, Santa Marina 17, 📞947451191 💻,
6. **H Camino de Rabé** (€72-80): 📶, Calle Alta, 📞601617639 💻

20.6 Hornillos del Camino A H 💻 Spanish: "little ovens [or kilns] of the Camino"
1. **A Municipal** (🛏32+, €13-15): 🐾 W, Plaza de la Iglesia, 📞689784681, 📅all year, basic
2. **A Alfar de Hornillo** (🛏20, €12): 🍴🐾 W D 📶, Cantarranas 8, 📞654263857 💻
3. **A H Meeting Point** (🛏32, €12/38/42): 🍴🐾 📶 ⊚, Cantarranas 3, 📞608113599 💻
4. **H De Sol a Sol** (€44/55): 🐾 W 🍽, Cantarranas 7, 📞649876091
5. **H Casa del Abuelo** (€50/60): W, Real 44, 📞661869618 💻

26.5 San Bol
A Arroyo de San Bol (muni, 🛏12, €10): 🍴, 📞628927317 💻, 📅Apr-mid Oct
A Fuente Sidres (🛏12, €16): 🍴 W D 📶, 📞686908486 💻, 3.4m after San Bol

31.3 Hontanas A H 🍴🛒, see next page

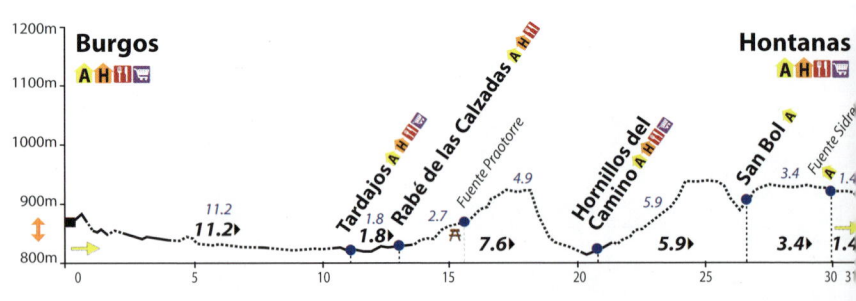

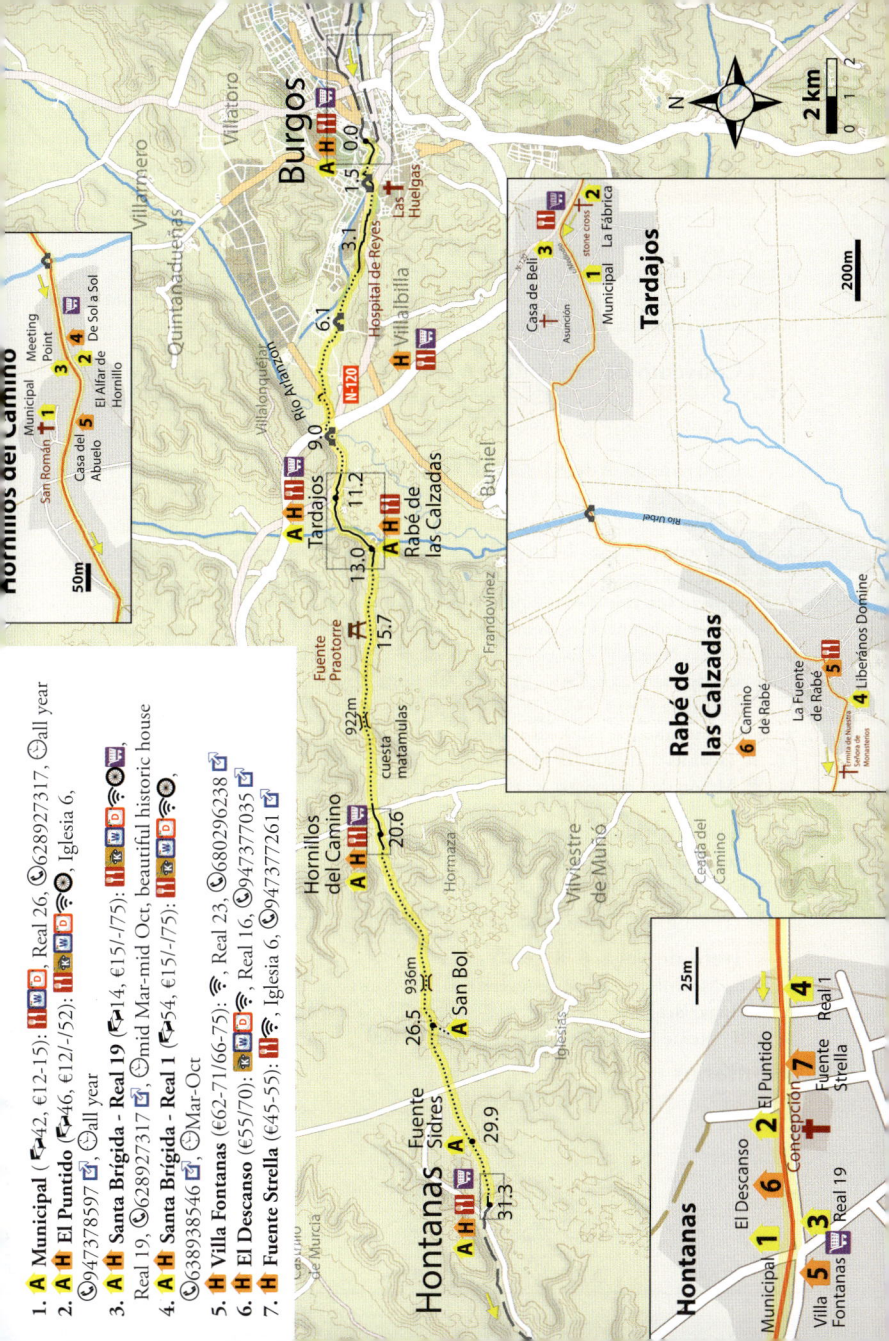

14 HONTANAS TO BOADILLA DEL CAMINO

28.4km (17.6mi), ▲ 272M / ▼ 357M, ⏱ 6-8 Hours
🅿 30%, 8.5km, 🆄 70%, 19.9km, **Difficulty:** ▬▬☐

💡 Most of this day is on pleasant dirt tracks with two towns offering pilgrim services. The hill after Castrojeriz is especially steep (both up and down), so be sure to reserve energy and take plenty of water for this shadeless section. After San Nicolás, the path crosses from Burgos province into Palencia. Note that Boadilla did not have a shop at time of research.

5.6 Convento de San Antón A Hospital de Peregrinos de San Antón
(⛌12, don): 🍴, ⏱Apr-Oct 📧, in ruins of convent, communal meals by candlelight, no electricity or hot water, basic, special experience

9.3 Castrojeriz A H A ▲ 🛒 ⛪ ✚ € ℹ 🏧 ℹ Plaza Mayor 3, ☎947377001
1. **A H** La Rinconada (⛌18, €14/-/50): 🆆 🅳 📶, Virgen del Manzano 4, ☎698942323 📧
2. **A H** Orion (⛌22, €14/45/55): 🍴 🅺 🅳 📶 ⊙, Colegiata 28, ☎649481609 📧
3. **A H** Ultreia (⛌28, €14/45/60): 🍴 🆆 🅳 📶 ⊙ ▲, Real de Oriente 77, ☎947378640
4. **A H** A Cien Leguas (⛌18, €14/42/62): 🍴 📶 ⊙, Real de Oriente 78, ☎947562305
5. **A** Espacio Interior (⛌5, €20): 🍴 🅺 🆆 ⊙, Real de Oriente 64, ☎623955375 📧, ⏱Apr-Nov, communal veg dinner, meditation sessions
6. **A H** Casa Nostra (⛌26, €15/-/40): 🅺 🆆 🅳 📶, Real Oriente 52, ☎947377493 📧
7. **A** San Esteban (asoc, ⛌30, €9): 🅺 📶 ⊙, Plaza Mayor, ☎947377001, ⏱a.y., historic
8. **A H** Rosalía (⛌32, €15/-/38): 🆆 🅳 📶, Cordón 2, ☎947373714 📧, ⏱Mar-Oct
9. **H** El Manzano (€45/55): 🆆 🅳 📶, Colegiata 5, ☎620782768
10. **H** Iacobus (€46/60): 🍴, Plaza Puerta del Monte, ☎947378647 📧
11. **H** Mesón de Castrojeriz (€36/50): 📶 ⊙, Cordón 1, ☎947377400 📧

18.3 San Nicolás Chapel A
A ⭐ San Nicolás (asoc, ⛌12, don): 🍴, ⏱Jun-Sep, to the L before the bridge, communal meals, 13th-century church restored and run by an Italian Confraternity, no electricity [except in bathroom/shower out back], ritual of foot washing

20.0 Itero de Vega A H 🍴 🛒 🏧
1. **A** La Mochila (⛌28, €12-15): 🍴 🅺 🆆 🅳 📶, Santa Ana 3, ☎979151781, ⏱all year
2. **A** Hogar del Peregrino (⛌8, €17): 🅺 🆆 🅳 📶, Santa María 17, ☎979151866
3. **A H** Puente Fitero (⛌22, €12-15/35/45): 🍴 🆆 🅳, Santa María 3, ☎979151822

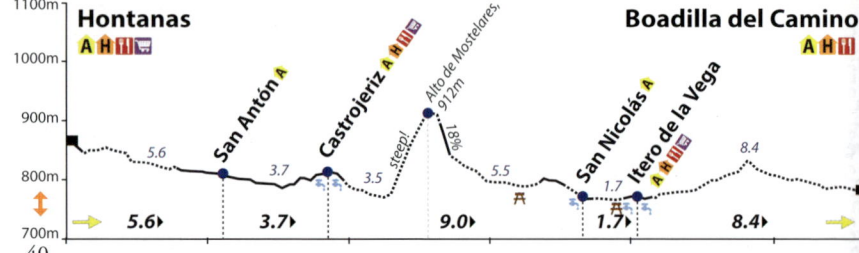

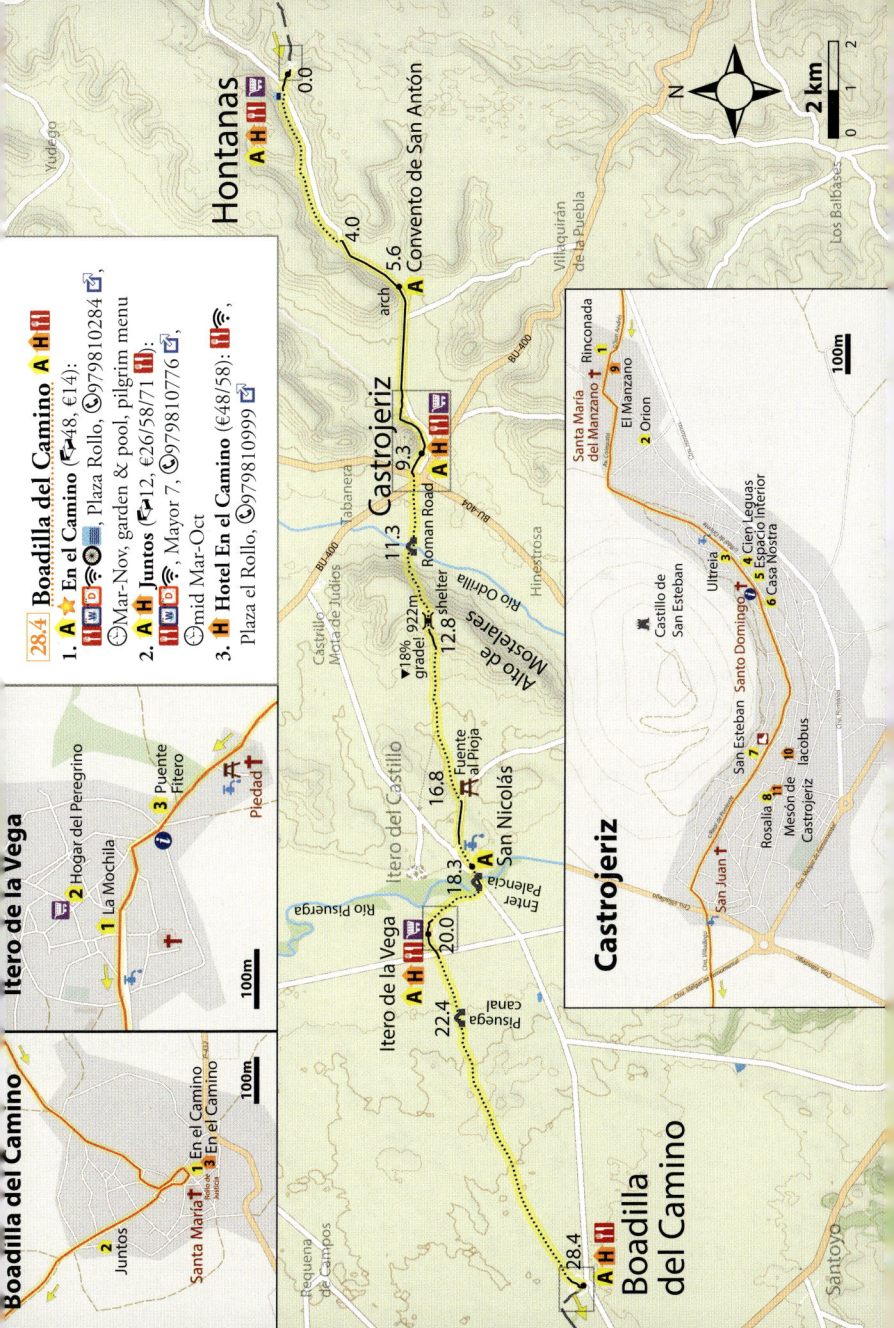

15

BOADILLA TO CARRIÓN DE LOS CONDES

24.7km (15.3mi), ▲ 164M / ▼ 111M, ⏱ 6-7 HOURS
🅿 18%, 4.4km, Ⓤ 82%, 20.3km, **DIFFICULTY:** ▬▬☐☐

☀ This day begins along the Canal de Castilla to Frómista before following along the road to Población. Next choose between two alternates, the more obvious and better-marked path along a gravel path parallel to the highway, or a river route that follows the small Río Ucieza and provides more shade and peace and quiet, but is not as well marked. The routes meet in Villalcázar for the last slog to Carrión parallel to the road.

5.8 Frómista A H 🍴 🛒 ➕ ℹ 📧 🚌
1. **A Municipal** (🛏56, €14): 🚿 W D 🍳, Plaza de San Martín, ☎979811089, 🗓Feb-Nov
2. **A Vicus** (🛏6, €14): 🚿 W D 📶, Ingeniero Rivera 25, ☎617483264, 🗓Mar-mid Dec
3. **A H Luz de Frómista** (🛏26, €13/20/34): 🚿 W 📶 🍳, Ejército Español 10, ☎635140169 📧, 🗓all year except Aug 1-20 and Christmas
4. **A Estrella del Camino** (🛏32, €17): 🍴 W D 📶, Ejército Español, ☎979810399 📧
5. **A Betania** (🛏9, don): Ejército Español 26, ☎638846043, 🗓**winter only, call ahead**
6. **H Hostal Camino de Santiago** (€60-75): 📶, Francesa 26, ☎979810282 📧
7. **H Hostal San Pedro** (€60-70): 🍴📶, Ejército Español 8, ☎979810016 📧
8. **H San Martín** (€60-70): 🍴📶, San Martín 7, ☎979810000 📧

9.2 Población de Campos A H 🍴 🛒
1. **A Municipal** (🛏18, €8): 🚿🍳, ☎979811099
2. **H Amanecer en Campos** (€40/55): 🍴📶, Fuente Nueva, ☎979811099 📧

14.9 Villarmentero A H 🍴
1. **A H Amanecer** (🛏36, dorm €10): 🍴🚿, José Antonio 2, ☎662-279102 📧, 🗓Mar-Oct
2. **H Casona Doña Petra** (€55): 🍴, Ramon y Cajal 14, ☎979-065978 📧

19.0 Villalcázar de Sirga A H 🍴 🛒
1. **A Casa del Peregrino** (🛏20, €10): 🚿 W D, Plaza Peregrino, ☎979888041, 🗓Apr-Oct
2. **A H Don Camino** (🛏20, €14/54/61): 🍴 W D 📶 🍳, Real 23, ☎979888163 📧
3. **H Hostal Las Cantigas** (€35/45): 🍴📶, Durango 2, ☎979888027 📧
4. **H Infanta Doña Leonor** (€45/55): 📶, Condes Toreno, ☎979888118 📧

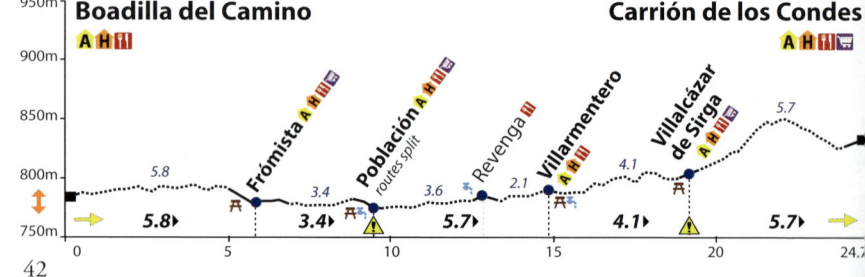

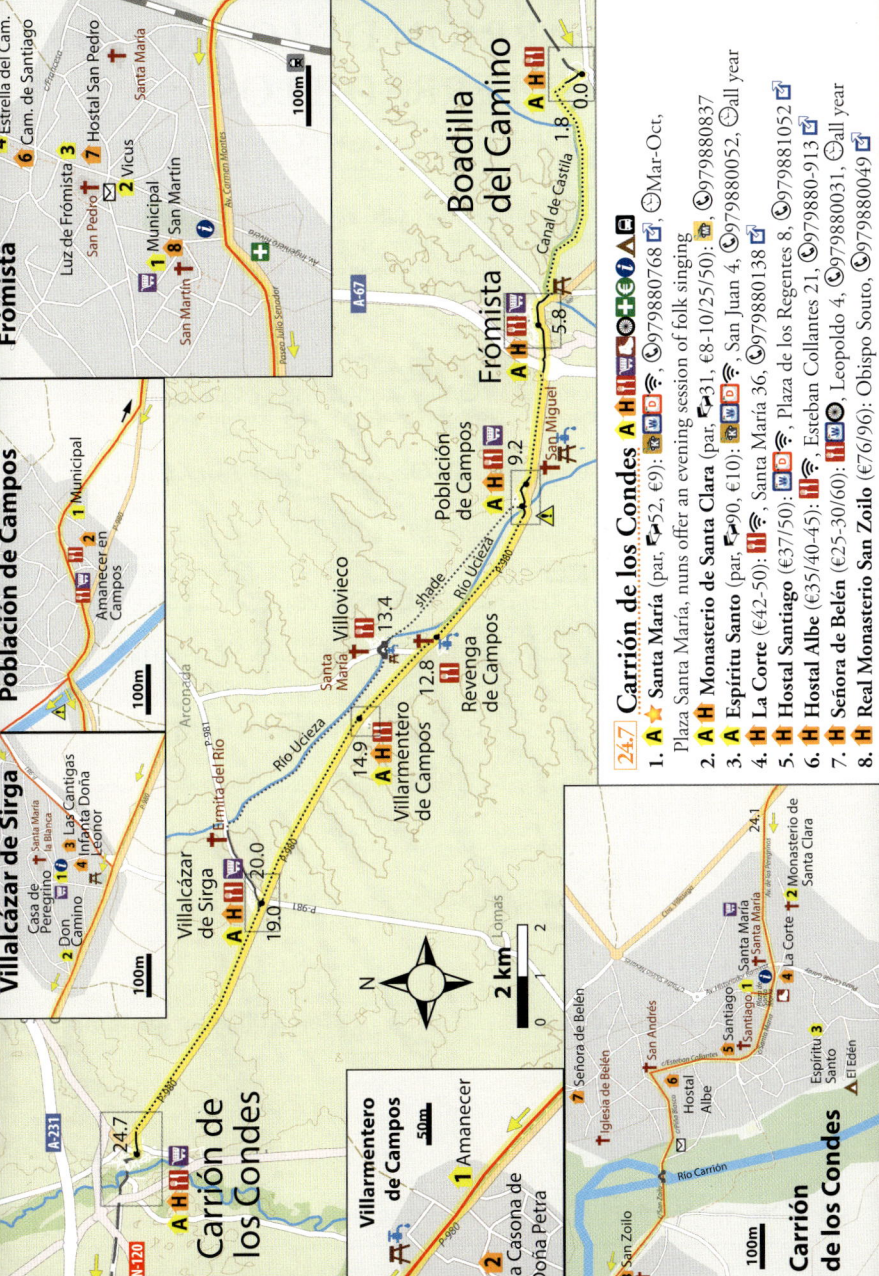

16

CARRIÓN DE LOS CONDES TO TERRADILLOS

26.5km (16.5mi), ▲ 175M / ▼ 127M, ⏱ 6-7 HOURS
🅿 29%, 7.7km, 🆄 71%, 18.8km, **DIFFICULTY:** ▰▱▱

💡 This day begins with a long, straight slog on the *Via Aquitana*, an ancient Roman route that has been restored. This is one of the longest stretches between towns on the Camino Francés: 17km to Calzadilla de la Cueza, no water sources and very minimal coverage for any bathroom breaks. The only respite is a seasonal snack stand offering drinks and sandwiches at about the halfway point to Calzadilla.

17.1 Calzadilla de la Cueza A H 🍴 🚍
1. **A Municipal** (🛏34, €10): W D 📶 ⊙, Mayor 1, ☎670558954, ⊙all year
2. **A H Los Canarios** (🛏11, €18-22/-/48): 🍴 📶 ⊙, Mayor 2, ☎659976894 📝, ⊙Easter-Oct
3. **A Camino Real** (🛏80, €10-15): 🍴 W D ⊙ 🚍, Mayor 8, ☎979883187, ⊙all year, call for the lower €10 rate
4. **H Camino Real** (€46/58): 🍴, Travesía Mayor 5, ☎979883187

23.3 Ledigos A H 🍴 🛒 🚍
1. **A H El Palomar** (🛏52, €12/-/30): 🍴 🔑 🛒 W 📶 ⊙ 🚍, Ronda de Abajo, ☎979883605, ⊙Mar-Nov, bar/shop in albergue
2. **A H La Morena** (🛏37, €23/45/60): 🍴 🔑 W D 📶, Carretera 3, ☎626972118 📝

26.5 Terradillos de los Templarios A H 🍴 🚍
1. **A H Los Templarios** (🛏52, €13/32/42): 🍴 W D 📶 🚍, ☎667252279 📝, ⊙late Mar-Oct
2. **A Jacques de Molay** (🛏49, €12-15): 🍴 🛒 W D 📶 ⊙, Iglesia, ☎979883679, ⊙Feb-Nov

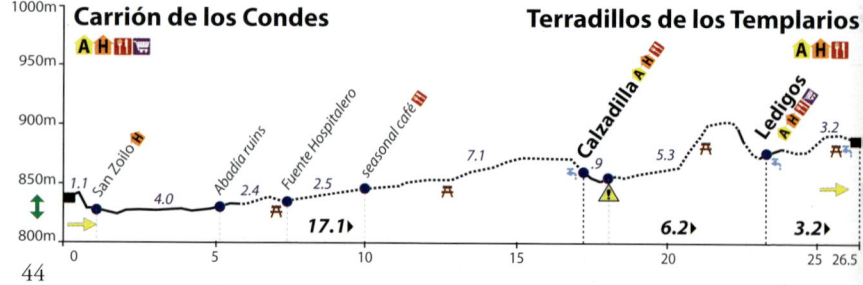

17

TERRADILLOS TO CALZADILLA

26.5km (16.5mi), ▲ 221M / ▼ 215M, ⏱ 5.5-7 Hours
🅿 19%, 5.0km, Ⓤ 81%, 21.5km, **Difficulty:** ▬◻◻

💡 From Terradillos to Sahagún, the trail largely parallels the N-120 road through Meseta scenery and small towns with mudbrick houses. Sahagún has a wealth of historic buildings. At the split in Calzada de Coto, choose between the more remote northern route along the Roman *Via Trajana* to Calzadilla (recommended) or stay on the southern *Real Francesa* route, which parallels the paved road on a gravel track.

3.3 Moratinos A H 🍴 🛒
1. **A H San Bruno** (asoc, 🛏32, €15/-/50): 🍴Ⓦ📶, Ontanón 9, ☎979061465 ✉, ⏱Apr-Jan, run by Italian Association
2. **A H Moratinos** (🛏10, €13-14/40-45/50-60): 🍴ⓌⒹ📶, Real 12, ☎979061466 ✉, ⏱all year
3. **H El Castillo de Moratinos** (€32/40): 🍴📶🅿, Real 10, ☎669320501 ✉

6.0 San Nicolás del Real Camino A 🍴 🛒
A Laganares (🛏20, €16): 🍴ⓌⒹ📶🅿, Plaza Iglesia, ☎979188142 ✉, ⏱Mar 15-Oct

13.3 Sahagún A H 🍴🛒🏧➕🏥ℹ🔺🚌🚆
1. **A Cluny** (muni, 🛏64, €7): 🅺ⓌⒹ, Arco 78, ☎987782117, ⏱a.y., smaller in winter
2. **A Sahagún** (🛏4, €18/30/50): 📶🅿, Arco 66, ☎613486529 ✉
3. **A Viatoris** (🛏50, €8-10): 🅺ⓌⒹ📶🅿, Arco 25, ☎987780975 ✉, ⏱Mar-Oct, bike rental
4. **A H Santa Cruz** (par, 🛏68, €7/25/30): 🅺Ⓦ📶, Antonio Nicolas 40, ☎650696023 ✉, shared meal, pilgrim Mass & blessing
5. **H Domus Viatoris** (€45/60): 🍴📶, Ctra. Sahagún-Arriondas, ☎987780975 ✉
6. **H La Codorniz** (€43/55): 🍴📶, Constitución 97, ☎987780276 ✉
7. **H Alfonso VI** (€35/40): 📶, Antonio Nicolás 4, ☎987781144 ✉
8. **H Los Balcones del Camino** (€54/60): Ⓦ📶, Constitución 53, ☎676838242
9. **H Escarcha** (€25/40): Regina Franco 12, ☎987781856
10. **H El Ruedo II** (€35-40/55-60): 🍴, Plaza Mayor 1, ☎987781834 ✉

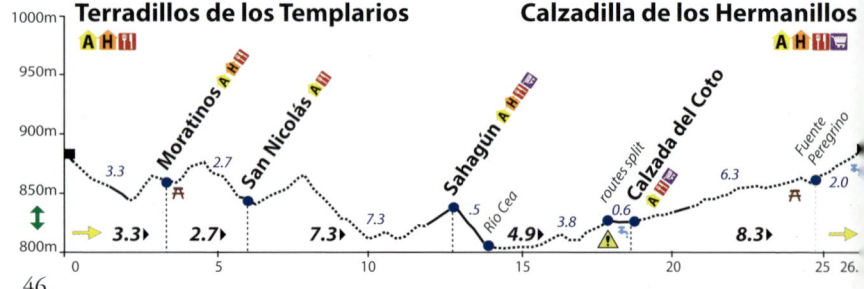

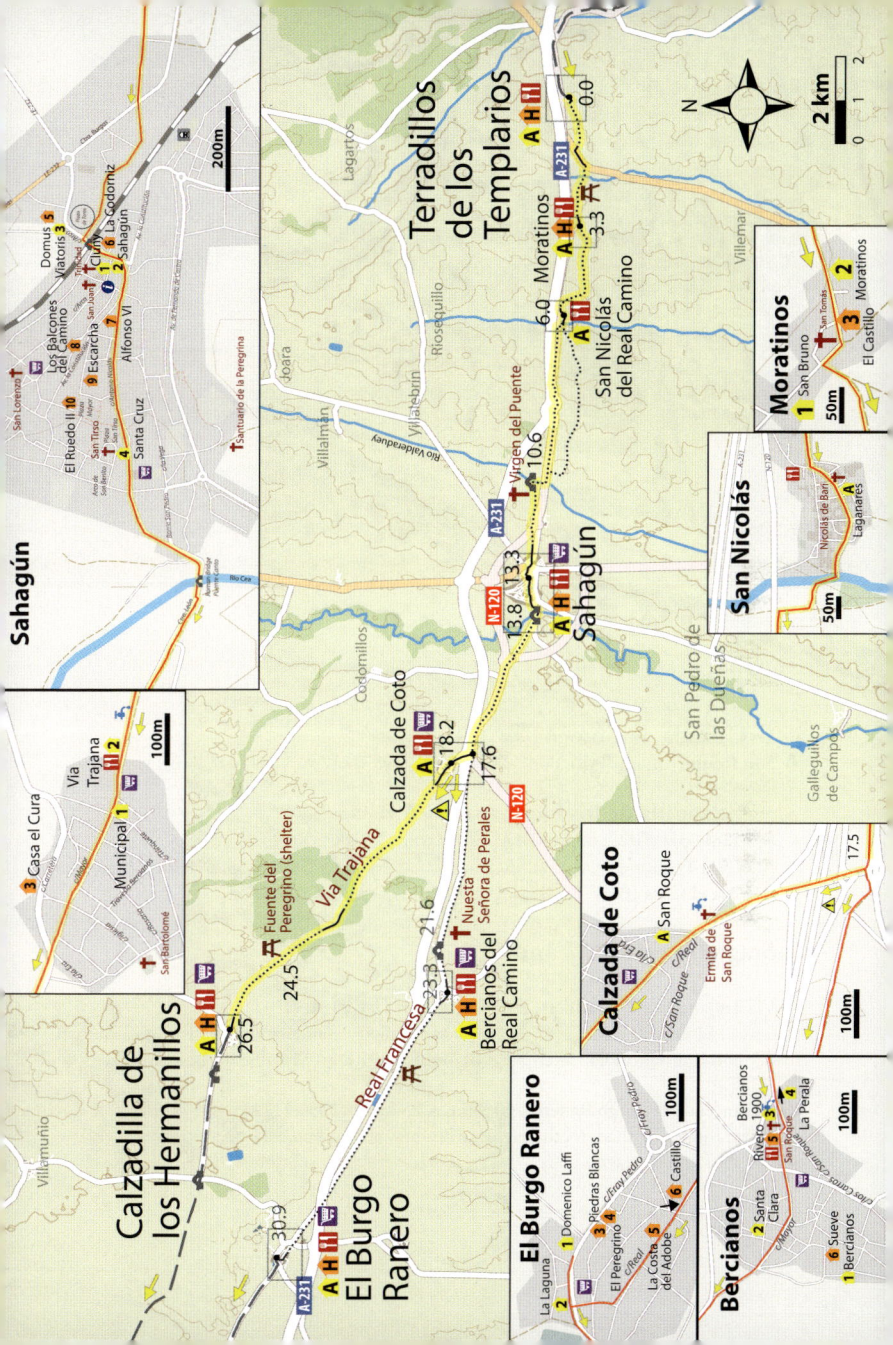

Walking parallel to the road on the alternate route

18.2 Calzada de Coto A 🍴🛒
A San Roque (muni, ⌂36, don): 🚿W, Real, ©987781233, ⊙all year, basic, key in bar

26.5 Calzadilla de los Hermanillos A H 🍴🛒
1. **A Municipal** (⌂22, don): 🚿W D 📶, Mayor 1, ©987330023, ⊙all year
2. **A H Via Trajana** (⌂10, €20/45/50): 🍴W D, Mayor 55, ©987337610 🗺, ⊙Apr-Nov
3. **H Casa el Cura** (€68/78): 🍴W, Carretera 13, ©987337647 🗺

⚠ Stage Options: 17 and 17A

⭐ **Via Trajana (via Calzadilla), 26.5km, ▲ 221M / ▼ 215M (17)**
Recommended as the route is farther from the highway, more remote and follows a Roman road. Shorter distance than alternate, but **4.4km farther** to Mansilla in the next stage.

Real Francesa (via Burgo Ranero), 30.9km, ▲ 234M / ▼ 233M (17A)
Alternate route that shadows the highway but has more intermediary services (see p. 49). Allows shorter next stage.

Routes reconvene in Reliegos on stage 18 (p. 50).

⚠ **Alternate Stages 17A-18A: Real Francesa**
17A: Terradillos to Burgo Ranero, 30.9km, ▲ 234M / ▼ 233M,
18A: Burgo Ranero to Mansilla (via Reliegos), 19.3km, ▲ 55M / ▼ 135M,
*distances measured from Terradillos

STAGE 17A: P 15%, 4.5km , U 85%, 26.4km
STAGE 18A: P 12%, 2.2km, U 88%, 17.0km

23.3 Bercianos del Real Camino A H ¶ 🛒
1. **A** ⭐ **Bercianos** (par, ⛌46, don): ¶, S. Rita 11, ☏987784008, ⊙Apr-Oct, meals/singing, +500m
2. **A H Santa Clara** (⛌10, €15/40/45): 🅺¶ⓌⒹ📶, Iglesia 3, ☏605839993, ⊙all year
3. **A Bercianos 1900** (⛌20, €18): ¶ⓌⒹ📶⊙, Mayor 49, ☏669282824 📝, ⊙Mar-Nov
4. **A H La Perala** (€15/38/48): ¶ⓌⒹ📶⊙, ☏685817699, ⊙all year, 750m before town
5. **H Rivero** (€40-50/47-55): Mayor 12, ☏987784287 📝
6. **H Sueve** (35/45): ¶📶, Iglesia 21, ☏987784139

30.9 El Burgo Ranero A H ¶ 🛒 ✚ 🚌 ☒
1. **A Domenico Laffi** (muni, ⛌28, don): 🅺ⓌⒹ, Plaza Mayor, ☏987330023 📝, ⊙all year
2. **A H La Laguna** (⛌18, €12-15/30/40): 🅺ⓌⒹ, Laguna 12, ☏987330094, ⊙Mar-Nov
3. **H Piedras Blancas** (€35/45): ¶ⓌⒹ, Fray Pedro 32, ☏987330094
4. **H El Peregrino** (€35/50): ¶ⓌⒹ, Fray Pedro 36,☏987330069
5. **H La Costa del Adobe** (€35/48): ¶ⓌⒹ📶⊙, Real 69, ☏676550508 📝, ⊙Apr-Nov
6. **H Hotel Castillo** (€32/55): ¶📶, Autovía km 34, ☏987330403 📝

Mudbrick albergue Domenico Laffi in Burgo Ranero

18 CALZADILLA TO MANSILLA DE LAS MULAS

23.8km (14.8mi), ▲ 81M / ▼ 171M, ⏱ 6-7 Hours
P 24%, 5.7km, **U** 76%, 18.1km, **Difficulty:** ▬▬▭

☀ This is an isolated day, far from towns and paved roads, along one of the best sections of Roman road in all of Spain. Be sure to bring sufficient water and food for the 17.6km without services until Reliegos, where this route joins the southern route from El Burgo Ranero (details in stage 17) and continues into Mansilla parallel to a paved road.

17.6 Reliegos A H 🍴
1. **A Municipal** (🛏45, €9): 🍳, Escuela, ☎987317801, ⊙all year
2. **A H La Parada** (🛏36, €12/-/40): 🍴🛏W D 📶, Escuela 7, ☎987317880, ⊙Jan-Dec 20, small 🛒
3. **A H Gil** (🛏14, €13/-/35): 🍴🛏W D 📶, Cantas 30, ☎987317804, ⊙Easter-Nov
4. **A H Las Hadas** (🛏20, €23/52/62 🔲): 🍴W 📶, Real 42, ☎620547454 ✉, ⊙Mar-Oct, vegetarian
5. **A H Vive tu Camino** (🛏20, €13/55/65): 🍴🛏W D 📶, Real 56, ☎610293986 ✉, ⊙Mar-Oct
6. **H Cantina de Teddy** (€60/80): 🍴🛏W D 📶, Cantas, ☎987190627 ✉, ⊙Mar-Oct

23.8 Mansilla de las Mulas A H 🍴🛒➕💊ℹ️📮 🛈 Plaza Pozo 12, ☎987310012
1. **A Municipal** (🛏18, €7): 🛏W ⊙, Av. Picos de Europa 32, ☎692970008, ⊙1pm all year, provisional while new albergue under construction
2. **A El Jardín del Camino** (🛏32, €16-20): 🍴🛏W D 📶⊙, Camino de Santiago 1, ☎987310232 ✉, ⊙all year, call in winter
3. **A Gaia** (🛏18, €12): 🍳W D 📶, Constitución 28, ☎699911311 ✉, ⊙a.y. except Feb
4. **H Pensión de Blanca** (€33-43/48): 📶, Picos de Europa 4, ☎626003177 ✉
5. **H Hostal San Martín** (€30/45): 🍴📶, Picos de Europa 32, ☎987310094
6. **H La Casa de los Soportales** (€68): 📶, Plaza Arrabal 9, ☎987310232 ✉
7. **H Albergueria del Camino** (€38/56): 🍴, Concepción 12, ☎987311193 ✉
8. **H Casadidoru** (€30/50-60): 📶, de los Mesones 20, ☎661496097 ✉

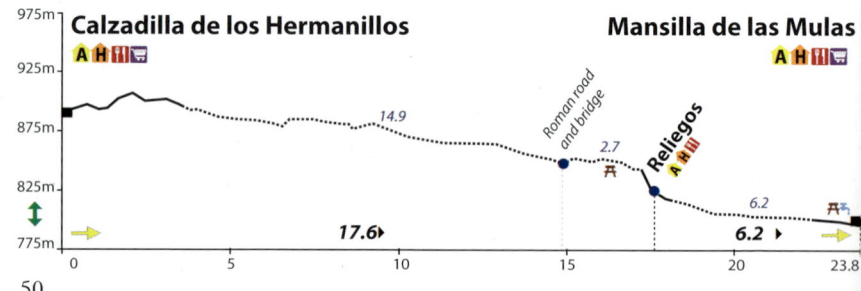

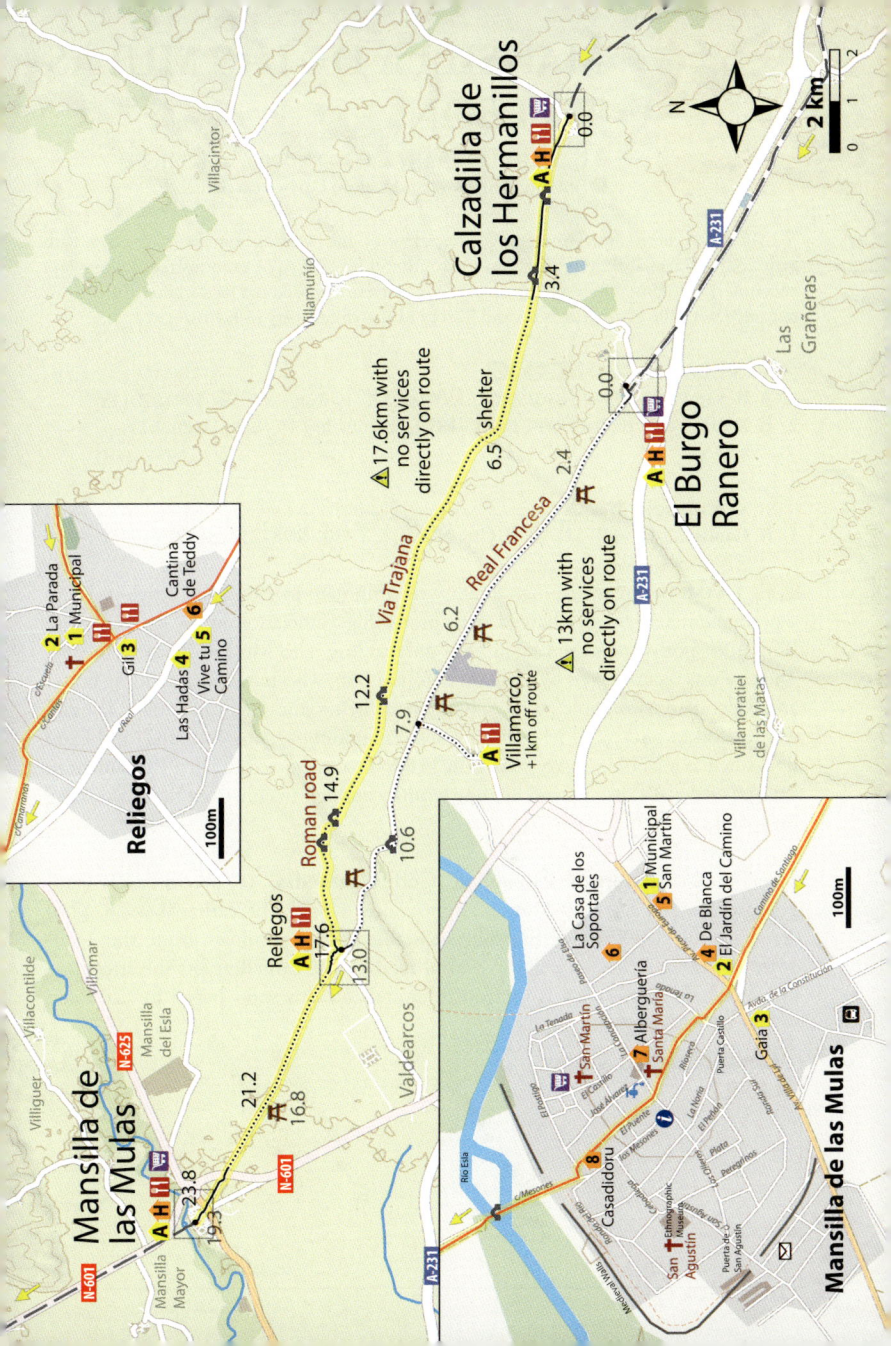

19 MANSILLA DE LAS MULAS TO LEÓN

18.1km (11.2mi), ▲ 153M / ▼ 120M, ⏱ 4-5 Hours
🅿 38%, 6.9km, 🆄 62%, 11.2km, **Difficulty:** ▬◻◻

💡 Much has been done to improve the safety of the walking approach to León with pedestrian bridges and overpasses, but the route still involves a lot of industrial walking and encounters with busy highways. Be on alert for trail markers, detours, and traffic! The effort is rewarded with the fascinating sites and history of the vibrant city of León.

6.0 Villarente A H ⅋ 🛒 ✚ 🟢 🅱
1. **A H San Pelayo** (🛏56, €15/50/68): 🍴 ♿ W D 🛜, El Romero 9, 📞650918281 📝
2. **H Delfín Verde** (€30-42/60-72): 🍴 🛜 ▬ 🟢, Crta 601 km 15, 📞987312065 📝, ⏱Mar-Oct

10.4 Arcahueja H ⅋ 🅱
1. **H Camino Real** (€47-52): 🍴 🛜, Ctra N-601, km 320, 📞987218134 📝, +400m

18.1 León began as a Roman military encampment in 29CE and developed into a permanent settlement charged with protecting Galician gold on its journey to Rome. Visigoths took the city in 585, only to lose it to Muslim invaders in 712. The city was reconquered by Ordoño I around 850, who initiated a building boom and welcomed Mozárabic refugees (Christians living under Muslim rule). The city was leveled in 988 by Al-Mansur's troops. Rebuilding began soon after, and León flourished as a wool industry center. In 1188, the city hosted the first Parliament in Europe under Alfonso IX and became wealthy enough to construct the astonishing cathedral.

León's finest treasure is its sublime Gothic **cathedral** (€7, ⏱M-Sa 9:30am-1:30pm, 4-8pm Su 9:30-11am, 2-8pm/winter closed 1hr earlier 📞987875770 📝) featuring 1,800m^2 of magnificent stained glass windows from the 13th-15th centuries. Without a flashy central retablo, the cathedral lets the streaming light steal the show. This is the fourth church on this spot, began in 1205 and

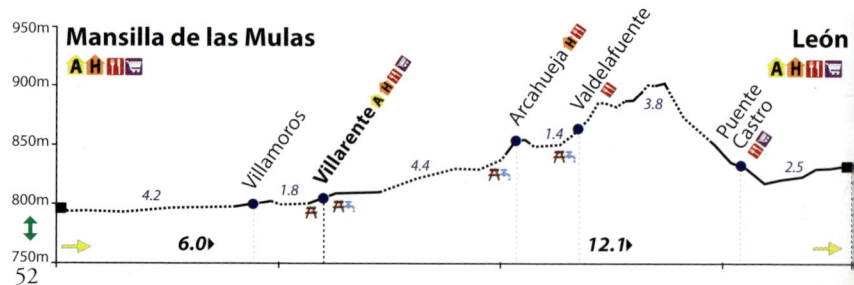

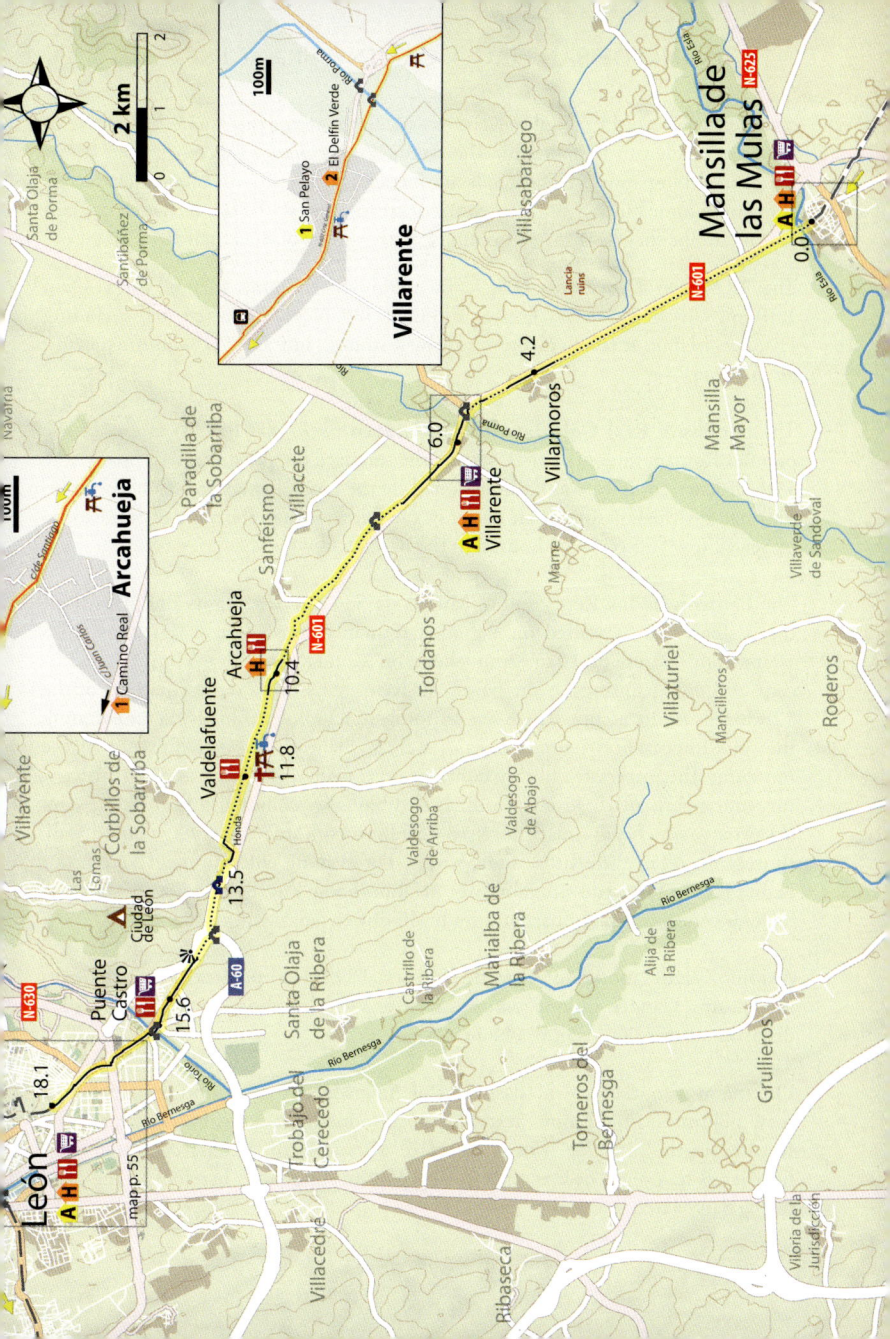

CAMINO DE SANTIAGO: CAMINO FRANCÉS

completed in record time (about 100 years). From across the square, the whole of the west façade can be taken in. The serene *Virgen Blanca* welcomes from below the central tympanum. Choir stalls are intricately carved with biblical characters along with some humorous depictions of creative vices. The seven chapels contain Gothic tombs such as that of Ordoño II, with a scene of the crucifixion.

The **Museo Diocesano** (€5, Tu-S 9:30am-1:30pm, 4-7pm, Su 9:30am 1:30pm, closed Mondays) houses almost 1,500 pieces of sacred art, including Hispano-Islamic textiles, Hebrew funerary stones, and a 1576 sculpture, *Christ on the Cross*.

The impressive **Real Colegiata de San Isidoro** (987876161) is one of the premier Romanesque structures, setting the standard for all of northern Spain. The 11th-century complex was commissioned by the pious Fernando I to house relics returned by Muslims after their defeat in the Reconquista. The relics of San Isidoro of Seville (ca. 560-636) are housed in the basilica.

The **Panteón de los Reyes** and **Museo de San Isidoro**, across the plaza from the basilica, can be visited on a guided tour in Spanish (€5, June-Oct: Tu-S 10am-2pm, 5-8pm, Su 10am-2pm, closed on Mondays, winter 4-7pm). The 12th-century fresco paintings in the pantheon have remarkable representations of the 12 months on its arches. There are 44 tombs, including 23 kings, demonstrating the site's importance. Doña Urraca's jeweled chalice is another must-see of the museum. The impressive library contains texts from as far back as the 10th century and a particularly lovely illuminated Bible. The basilica also features a *Puerta del Perdón,* which pilgrims who were unable to continue to Santiago could walk through to receive substitute indulgences. For evening entertainment, check out León's **Barrio Húmedo** (literally "wet neighborhood") in the Old City, known for its high concentration of bars and tradition of free tapas with drinks.

Antonio Gaudí's modernist **Casa de Botines** (1893) incorporates Gothic elements but retains Gaudí's unique whimsical style. The building originally housed a department store and is now a bank.

On the way out of town, pass **Hostal San Marcos**, a sumptuous 15th-century pilgrim hospital now restored as a modern Parador hotel, which was featured in the film *The Way* as the place where Martin Sheen's character treats his friends to a night of luxury. A dozing pilgrim statue rests barefoot in the plaza facing San Marcos.

León

p 134,305. In Spanish, *León* means "lion," but the name comes from the Latin military term for legion.

A Benedictinas Carbajales (par, ☎132, €10): 🍴 W D 🛜, Plaza Santa María del Camino, ☎987252866, ⊙all year, evening Mass and pilgrim blessing, stuffy dorms, separate gender dorms

A H San Francisco de Asis (par, ☎100+, €12-18/49/55): 🍴 W D 🛜 ⊙, Alcalde Miguel Castaños 4, ☎987215060, ⊙all year

A Check In León (☎40, €12): K W D 🛜, Alcalde Miguel Castaño 88, ☎987498793, ⊙all year

A H S. Tomás Canterbury (☎54, €12-15/-/50): K W D 🛜, Lastra 53, ☎987392626, ⊙Feb-Nov

A Covent Garden Hostel (☎24, €22-25/-/35): K 🛜, Ancha 25, ☎987004428

⚠ A Miguel Unamuno (☎86, €13-18): W D 🛜, Pelayo 15, ☎987233010, ⊙July-Sept,

Closed for renovations 2024, reopening unknown

A H León Hostel (☎14, €22/55/55): K 🛜, Ancha 8, 987079907, ⊙all year

A Globetrotter Hostel (☎40, €15-20): W 🛜, Paloma 8, ☎987103267

A H Muralla Leonesa (☎65, €16/-/45): K W D 🛜, c/Tarifa 5, ☎987-177873, ⊙Mar-Oct

. H Hospedería San Fernando I (€63-77): 🍴 🛜, Cubos 32, ☎987220731

. H Hotel La Posada Regia (€66/78): 🍴 🛜, Regidores 9, ☎987213173

. H Guzmán el Bueno (€47/62): 🛜, Lopez Castrillón 6, ☎987236412

. H Hostal San Martín (€48/58): 🛜, Plaza de Torres de Omaña 1, ☎987875187

. H Pensión Blanca (€45/55): K W D 🛜 ⊙, Villafranca 2, ☎987251991

. H Parador Hostal de San Marcos (€300+): 🍴 🛜, Plaza San Marcos 7, ☎987237300, spa, luxurious, featured in "The Way" film, historic Renaissance building

Ciudad de León (tent €12, cabin €30/40): 🍴 W 🛜 🛒 🍽, ☎987269086, 3km out of city

20 LEÓN TO VILLAR DE MAZARIFE

22.0km (13.7mi), ▲ 225M / ▼ 181M, ⏱ 5-6 Hours
🅿 72%, 15.8km, Ⓤ 28%, 6.2km, **Difficulty:** ▬▢▢

💡 The exit from León is no more glamorous than the entrance with about 8km of city walking including some highly industrialized area. These can be skipped with bus A1 to Virgen de Camino, where the path leaves the León metro area. The path splits again, with the recommended route to the south and a northern route parallel to the N-120 road (20A León to Villadangos del Páramo 21.5km). The recommended route is longer but much more scenic. The routes converge in Hospital and again before Astorga.

4.5 Trobajo del Camino

- **El Abuelo** (€60-65): 🍴 📶, Los Mesones 6, ☎987801044
- **Hotel Alfageme** (€45/55): 🍴 Ⓦ 📶, Alfageme 55, ☎987840490, pilgrim rate

8.3 Virgen del Camino

1. **Don Antonino y Doña Cinia** (muni, ⛺40, €7-10): 🅺 Ⓦ Ⓓ 📶, Eustoquio 16, ☎ 987302800, 🕙Apr-Oct
2. **Hostales San Froilán and Plaza** (€50/65): 🍴 📶, Peregrinos 1, ☎987302019
3. **Hostal Central** (€35/52-58): 📶, Av. de Astorga 85, ☎987302041
4. **Hostal Julio Cesar** (€38/55): 🍴 📶, Cervantes 6, ☎987790220
5. **Villapaloma** (€40/55): 🍴 Ⓦ 📶, Astorga 47, ☎987300990
6. **Hostal Soto** (€49/72): 📶, Crta km 5, ☎987802925

12.1 Oncina de la Valdoncina

- **El Pajar** (⛺9, €12/-/38): 🅺 📶 ⊙, Arriba 4, ☎677567309, 🕙11am all year
- **Domus Oncinae** (€45-76): 🍴 📶, Real 7, ☎606803957

22.0 Villar de Mazarife

1. **S. Antonio de Pádua** (⛺50, €12-14/-/50): 🍴 Ⓦ Ⓓ, Leon 33, ☎987390192
2. **Casa de Jesús** (⛺60, €10): 🍴 🅺 Ⓦ, Corujo 11, ☎987390697, 🕙all year
3. **Tío Pepe** (⛺26, €12/45/55): 🍴 Ⓦ 📶, El Teso 2, ☎987390517, 🕙Mar-Nov

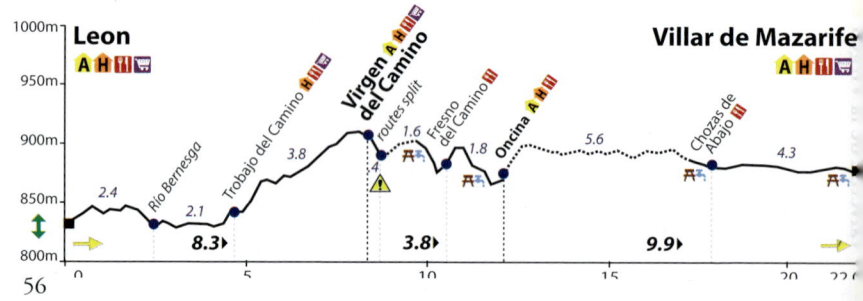

21

VILLAR DE MAZARIFE TO ASTORGA

31.8km (19.8mi), ▲ **237m** / ▼ **250m**, ⏱ **7-9 Hours**
🄿 43%, 13.7km, 🄾 57%, 18.1km, **Difficulty:** ■■□

💡 Enjoy the last flat Meseta scenery before the path becomes rolling green in the Cantabrian Mountains. Hospital de Órbigo is a pleasant halfway point to enjoy medieval ambiance.

9.8 Villavante A H 🍴🛒

A H Santa Lucía (📞24, €12/-/38-50): 🍴⚡🅆🛜⊙. Doctor Vélez 17, ☎692107693 📧
H Molino Galochas (€40/55 🏠): 🍴⚡🅆🛜, ☎987388546 📧

15.0 Hospital de Órbigo A H 🍴🛒✚€▲🚌

1. **A** Karl Leisner (par, 📞90, €10): ⚡, Álvarez Vega 32, ☎987388444 ⊙all year
2. **A H** La Encina (📞16, €14/-/48): 🍴⚡🅆🛜, Suero de Quiñones, ☎987361087 📧
3. **A** Casa de los Hidalgos (€15-18/-/50-60): ⚡🅆🛜⊙, Vega 36, ☎699198755 📧
4. **A H** San Miguel (📞36, €14/-/40): ⚡🅆🛜⊙, Vega 35, ☎987388285 📧, ⊙Apr-Nv
5. **A H**⭐ Albergue Verde (📞26, €16/-/45): 🍴⚡🅆🛜, Fueros León 76, ☎689927926 📧
6. **H** B&B Puente de Órbigo (€69-77): ⚡🛜, Reguerón 2, ☎630149922 📧
7. **H** Don Suero de Quiñones (€65/85): Álvarez Vega 1, ☎987388238
8. **H** Cantón Plaza (€55/68): 🍴🛜, Santos Oliver 27, ☎987388896 📧
9. **H** El Caminero (€50/55-70): 🍴, Sierra Pambley 56, ☎987389020 📧
10. **H** Paso Honroso (€50/68): 🍴🛜, N-120 km 335, ☎987361010 📧

17.6 Villares de Órbigo A H 🍴🛒✚🚌

A H Villares de Órbigo (📞22, €15/-/40-55): ⚡🅆🛜⊙, Arnal 21, ☎987132935 📧
A H El Encanto (📞10, €18/55/60 🏠): ⚡🅆🛜, C. Santiago 23, ☎987388126 📧

20.3 Santibañez de Valdeiglesias A H 🍴

A Parroquial (📞20, €12): 🍴, Caromonte 3, ☎626362159, ⊙Mar-Oct, poor reviews
A H Camino Francés (📞14, €15/-/50): 🍴⚡🅆🛜, Real 68, ☎987361014, ⊙Apr-Oct
H L'Abilleiru (€60): 🍴⚡🅆🛜, Real 44, ☎615269057 📧

28.1 San Justo de la Vega H 🍴🛒🚌

H Hostal Juli (€35/55): 🍴🛜, Real 56, ☎987617632 📧

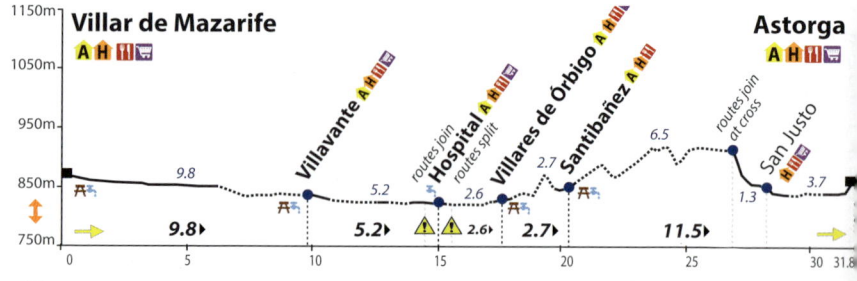

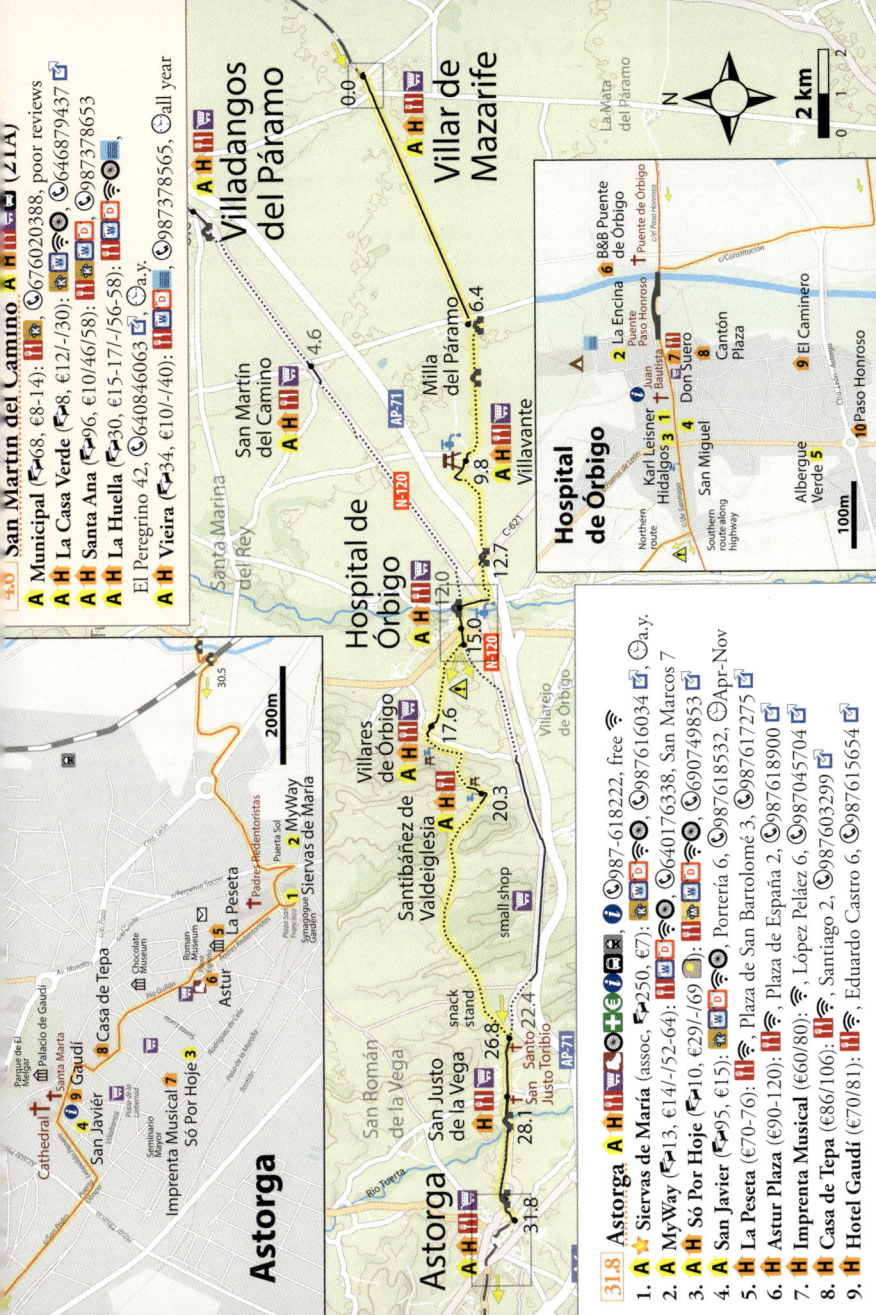

22

ASTORGA TO FONCEBADÓN

26.0km (16.2mi), ▲ **606m** / ▼ **49m**, ⊕ **6.5-8 Hours**
🅿 23%, 6.0km, Ⓤ 77%, 20.0km, **Difficulty:** ▬ ▬ ▬

💡 Today begins the slow steady climb toward the high point of the Camino Francés, reached in the following stage. The landscape and buildings change as the Camino draws nearer to the wild hills of Galicia. Vegetation becomes more scrubby, typical houses are low stone structures with thatch or slate roofs, and the weather becomes more dreary and overcast.

3.0 Valdeviejas A 🍴 🚌
A Ecce Homo (muni, 🛏10, €10): ♿ W D, 📞620960060, ⊕Mar-Oct, all beds not bunks

5.3 Murias de Rechivaldo A H 🍴 🚌
1. **A** Municipal (🛏14, €10): W, Crta Santa Colomba, 📞669067433, ⊕Mar-Oct
2. **A H** Las Águedas (🛏30, €15/-/55-60): W D 📶, C. Santiago 52, 📞636067840 🔗
3. **A H** Casa Flor (🛏15, €17/-/63): 🍴 📶, Santa Colomba 54, 📞609478323 🔗
4. **H** La Veleta (€60): 🍴 W 📶, Plaza Mayor 1, 📞616598133 🔗

5.3+ Castrillo de Polvazares H 🍴 🚌, +1.0km, 🍴 Casa Coscolo Maragato specialty
H Cuca la Vaina (€55/70): 🍴 📶, Jardín, 📞987691034 🔗
H El Rincón Maragoto (€50/60): 📶, Concha Espina 3, 📞690236733 🔗

9.6 Santa Catalina A H 🍴 🚌
1. **A H** El Caminante (🛏22, €15/30/45): 🍴 W D, Real 2, 📞987691098 🔗, ⊕all year
2. **A** La Bohéme (🛏10, donativo): ♿ 🍴 W, El Pozo 11, 📞658262257, ⊕Apr-Oct
3. **A H** San Blas (🛏20, €10/30/35-40): 🍴 W D, Real 11, 📞987691411, ⊕all year
4. **H** Vía Avis (€70/80): 📶, El Sol 21, 📞987199319 🔗

13.9 El Ganso A H 🍴
A Gabino (🛏30, €13): ♿ 🍴 W D 📶, Real 9, 📞660912823 🔗, ⊕Easter-Oct
A Sigo Mi Camino (🛏10, €10): 🍴 ☕, Camino Real 20, 📞647595252
H Gabino (€50-60/60-70): 📶, Real 36, 📞625318585 🔗

20.5 Rabanal del Camino A H 🍴 🛒, Small shop (closed in winter), see next page

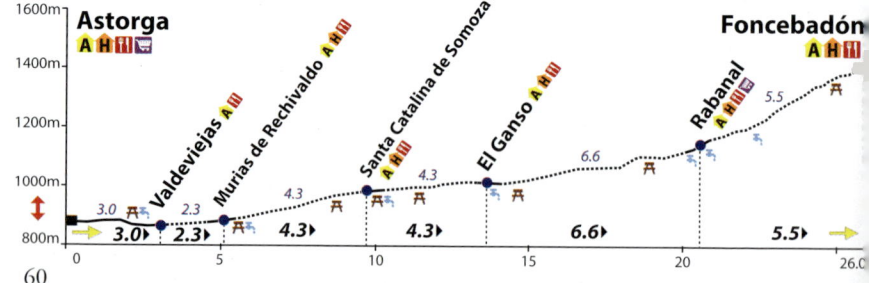

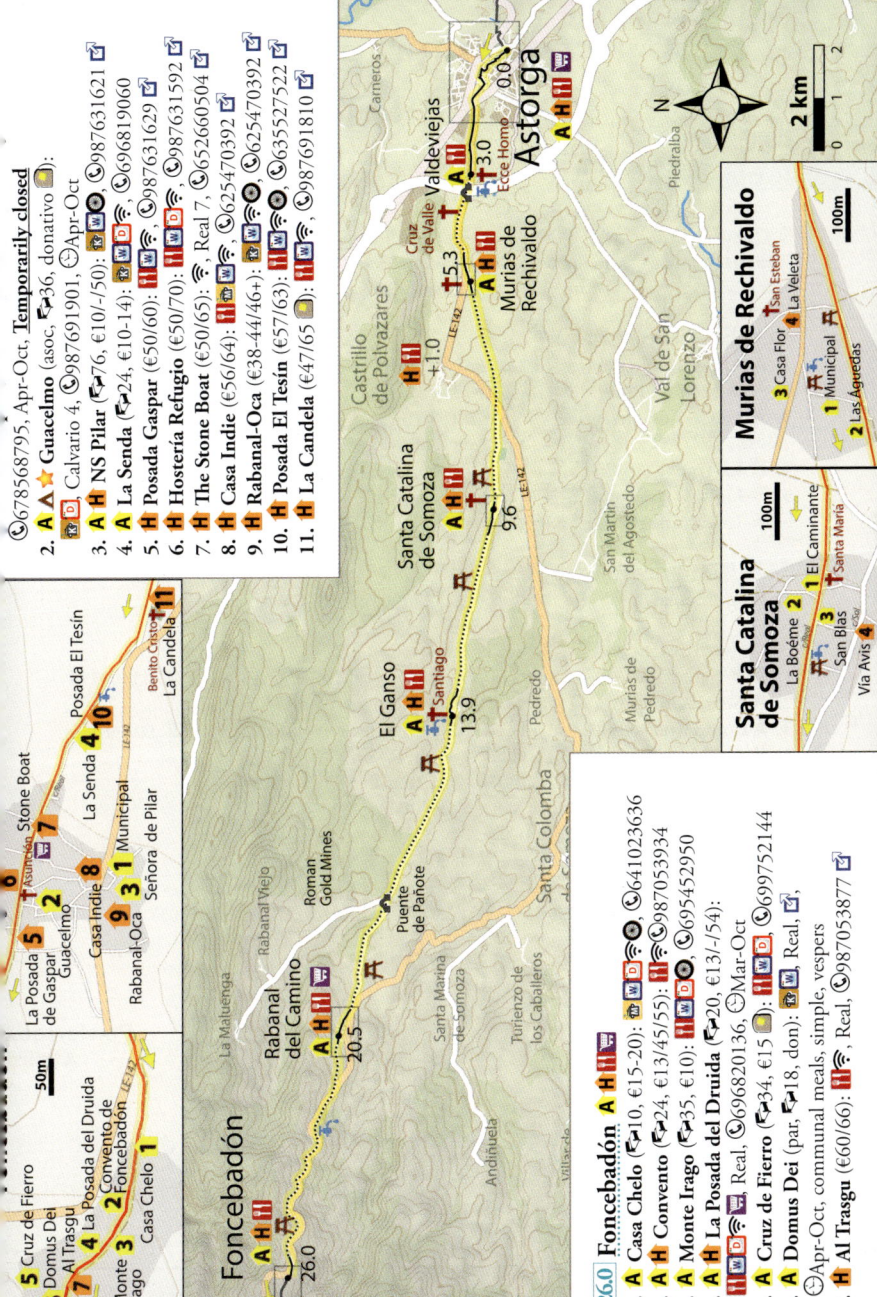

23

FONCEBADÓN TO PONFERRADA

27.0km (16.8mi), ▲ 231M / ▼ 1129M, ⏱ 6-8 Hours
🅿 27%, 7.3km, 🅤 73%, 19.7km, **DIFFICULTY:** ▬ ▪ ▪

💡 Climb to Cruz Ferro and the high point of the Irago Mountains before the steep descent to Ponferrada. Maragato mountain villages with slate-roofed houses like El Acebo offer services. The mountain views are superb on clear days. Be prepared for cold, rain, and wind.

11.2 El Acebo A H 🍴 🛒
1. **A Apóstal Santiago** (par, 🛏23, don): 🚻, Pl. Iglesia ⏱Apr-Oct, shared meals, vespers
2. **A H Mesón El Acebo** (🛏18, €12/-/35): 🍴 🚿 📶, Real 16, ☎987695074, ⏱Feb-Nov
3. **A La Casa del Peregrino** (🛏96, €20/55/70): 🍴 🚿 📶 ⊙, Crta Compludo, ☎987057793, ⏱Jan 10 - Dec 20, end of town
4. **H La Trucha** (€50/60): 🍴, La Cruz 10, ☎987695548, great vegetarian meals
5. **H La Rosa del Agua** (€47/51): 🚻, Real 52, ☎616849738
6. **H La Casa del Peregrino** (€55/70): 🍴 📶, Real 67, ☎987057875

14.7 Riego de Ambrós A 🍴
1. **A Municipal** (🛏30, €8): 🚿, Real, ☎640376118, ⏱Mar-Oct

19.5 Molinaseca A H 🍴 🛒 ✚ 🚌
1. **A H Santa Marina** (🛏38, €12/40/46): 🍴 🚿 ⊙ Manuel Fraga 55, ☎987453077
2. **A Señor Oso** (🛏16, €15): 🚻 🚿 📶 ⊙, Real 43, ☎661761970
3. **A Compostela** (🛏30, €12-14): 🍴 🚿 📶, Iglesia 39, ☎987453057, ⏱Apr-Nov
4. **H Casa Morrosco** (€30/42): 🍴 🚿, Pisón 6, ☎695679313
5. **H Casa del Reloj** (€45/50): 📶, ☎987453124
6. **H Pajarapinta** (€45/55): 🚿 📶, Real 30, ☎987453040
7. **H Casa San Nicolas** (€53/59): 🚻, 📶, La Iglesia 43, ☎534562008
8. **H Hostal el Horno** (€45/55): 📶, Rañadero 3, ☎987453203
9. **H El Palacio** (€53/59): 🍴 🚿 📶, El Palacio 19, ☎987453094
10. **H The Way Hostel** (€50-55/52-65): 🚿 📶, El Palacio 10, ☎637941017

27.0 Ponferrada A H 🍴 🛒 ✚ € 🚌 ℹ ☎987424236, see next page

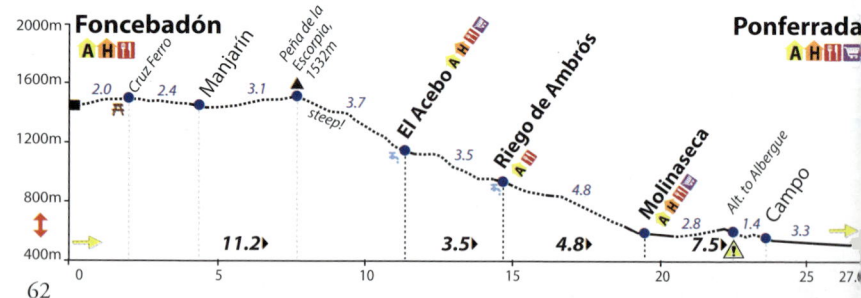

24

PONFERRADA TO VILLAFRANCA DEL BIERZO

24.4km (15.2mi), ▲ 273M / ▼ 259M, ⏱ 6-7 Hours
P 74%, 18.1km, U 26%, 6.3km, **Difficulty:** ▬ ☐ ☐

☀ Enter the Bierzo region with its temperate microclimate, ideal for viticulture. The scenery is green with vineyards, cherry orchards, wildflowers, and trees. The mountains of Galicia loom ahead, and beautiful Villafranca lies nestled among the foothills along the Río Burbia.

5.8 Columbrianos
- **H** Hotel Novo (€50/60): 📶, Ctra N-VI km 386, ☎987610630, <u>1km before town</u>
- **H** El Almendro de María (€55-60): 🅚📶, Real 56, ☎633481100

8.2 Fuentasnuevas
- **H** Hostal Monteclaro (€30/50): 🍴📶, Antonio Cortés 24, ☎987455982, <u>+1km</u>

10.6 Companaraya
- **A H** Medina (⛺20, €14/40/50): 🍴 W D 📶, Cam. Santiago 85, ☎987463962, 🕐all year
- **A** Naraya (⛺26, €10): 🍴📶, De Galicia 506, ☎987459159, 🕐Apr-Oct
- **H** Hostal Companaraya (€45/54): 📶, Camino de Santiago 50, ☎619279931
- **H** Hostal Orly (€28/45): Crta N-VI km 394, ☎98746302
- **H** La Casita B&B (€100 up to 4 people): 🅚📶, Plaza Constitución 35, ☎653736228

16.7 Cacabelos
1. **A H** Municipal (⛺70, €7): W D 📶, Pl. Santuario, ☎987547167, 🕐Apr-Oct, 2 beds/room
2. **A H** La Gallega (⛺30, €17/45/55): 🍴📶, Santa Maria 23, ☎987549476
3. **A H** El Molino (⛺14, €15/-/45): 🍴📶, María 10, ☎676690900, 🕐<u>closed Tues</u>
4. **A H** St. James Way (⛺10, €22/44/61): 🍴📶, Santa María 60-62, ☎987037871
5. **H** Santa María (€39/45-50): 🍴, Santa María 20, ☎987549588
6. **H** Hostal Siglo XIX (€47/62): 🍴📶, Santa María 2, ☎633422661
7. **H** Moncloa de San Lázaro (€70-129): 🍴W📶, Cimadevilla 97, ☎987546101

20.3 Valtuille de Arriba
- **A** Acogida La Biznaga (⛺6, don): 🅚W D, Platería 33, ☎682187093

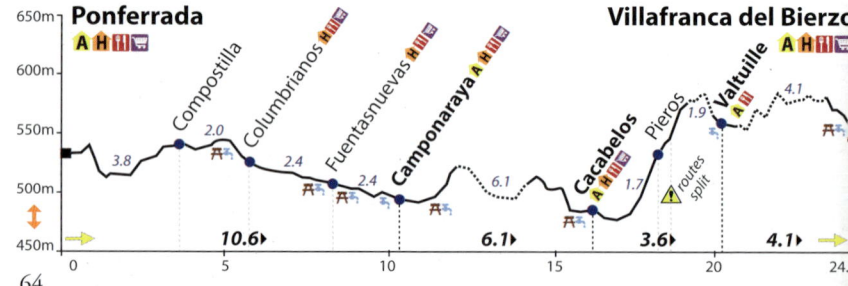

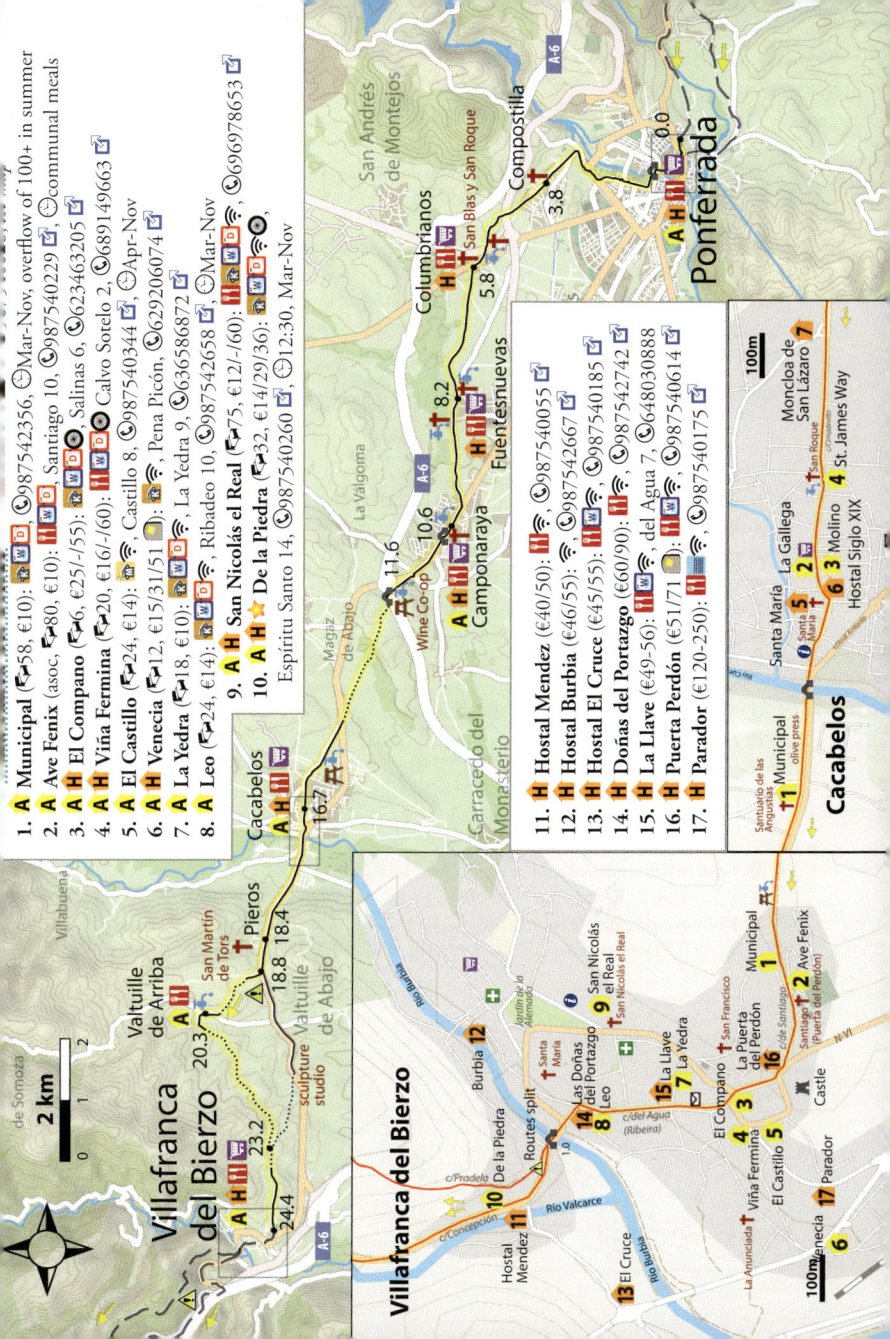

25

VILLAFRANCA TO LA FABA

23.8km (14.8mi), ▲ 534M / ▼ 183M, ⏱ 6-8 Hours
Ⓟ 94%, 22.4km, Ⓤ 6%, 1.4km, **Difficulty:** ▬▬▭

☀ While the trail doesn't officially enter Galicia until just before O Cebreiro, the culture, landscape, and architecture today all reflect Galician characteristics. Leaving Villafranca, the routes split with the more challenging but beautiful option to the R just before the bridge. While the flyover highway traffic can be distracting, the Valcarce Valley villages provide quaint respite. Save energy for the final uphill to La Faba along sometimes muddy or slippery trails.

5.6 Pereje H ⫽, H **Las Coronas** (€36/46): ☎987540138

10.0 Trabadelo A H ⫽ 🛒 ✚
1. A H **Municipal** (🛏18, €10/-/36): ⫽ ⚹ W D ⊙, ☎602321154
2. A H **Camino y Leyenda** (🛏8, €20/30/38): ⚹ W D 📶, ☎628921776 ✉, 🕐Apr-Oct
3. A H **Parroquial** (🛏22, €9/-/27): ⚹ W, Iglesia, ☎630628130 ✉, 🕐all year
4. A ⭐ **Casa Susi** (🛏10, €14): ⫽, Camino deSantiago 123, ☎675242114 ✉, 🕐Apr-Oct,
5. A **Crispeta** (🛏20, €12): ⫽ ⚹ W D 📶, Camino de Santiago, ☎620329386, 🕐all year
6. H **El Puente Peregrino** (€45-55): ⫽ 📶, Camino Santiago 153, ☎987566500
7. H **Nova Ruta** (€45/60): ⫽ 📶, ☎987566431 ✉
8. H **Os Arroxos** (€45/50): ⫽ ⚹ 📶 🚌, Camino de Santiago, ☎987566529 ✉, jacuzzi

14.1 Portela de Valcarce A H ⫽ 🛒 🚌
A H **El Peregrino** (🛏28, €12/28/38): ⫽ W D 📶 ⊙, ☎987543197 ✉, 🕐Mar-Oct
A **Vagabond Vieiras** (🛏4, €15): ⫽ ⚹ W D 📶 ⊙, Ctra N-VI 1, ☎669329821 ✉
H **Valcarce** (€42/66): ⫽ 📶 🚌, Autovia A-6, ☎987543180

15.4 Ambasmestas A H ⫽ 🚌
A H **Casa del Pescador** (🛏34, €10-12/22/30): ⫽ ⚹ W D 📶 🚌, Crta N-VI,
☎603515868 ✉, 🕐mid Mar-mid Nov, vegetarian meals
A H **Rincón Apóstol** (🛏16, €17/30-40/40-50 🍴): ⫽ W D 📶, N-VI 1, ☎987543099 ✉
H **CTR Ambasmestas** (€46/61): ⫽ 📶, Antigua VI 19, ☎987543247 ✉, 🕐all year

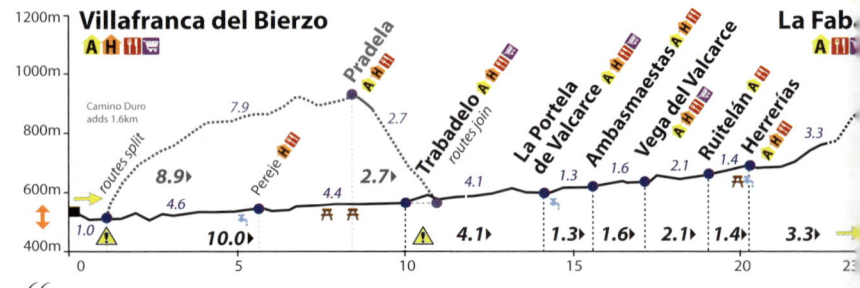

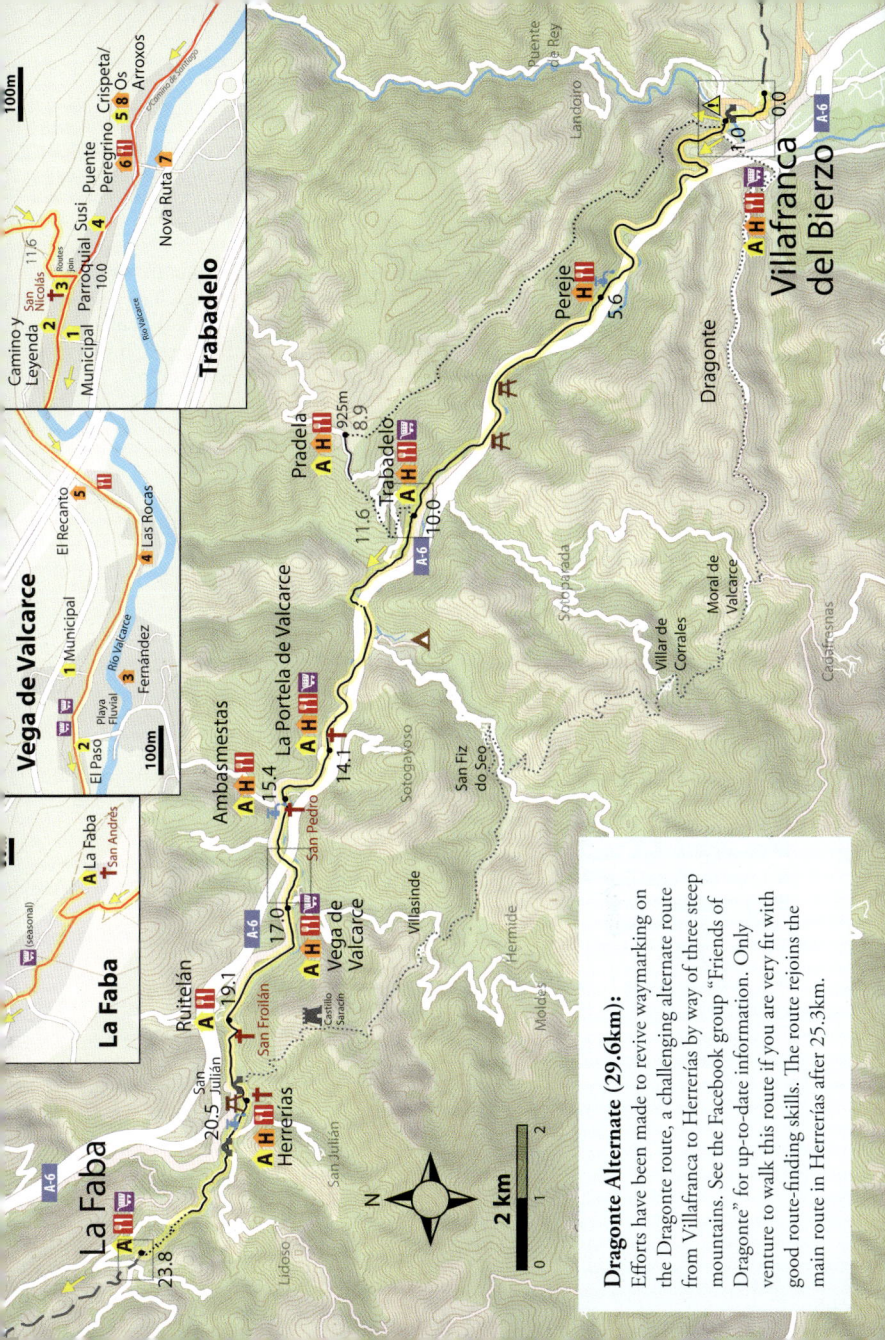

CAMINO DE SANTIAGO: CAMINO FRANCÉS

⚠ Route Options:

Primary highway route, 23.8km; This shorter and more popular route is entirely paved and on the shoulder of a highway next to a crash barrier all the way to Trabadelo.

Alternate high route "Camino Duro," 25.3km (p. 69); While this route is 1.6km longer and climbs much more in elevation than the highway route, the effort is rewarded with stunning views and earthen paths. Rejoins alternate route in 10.6km. 💡 The Camino Duro route option reduces stage 25 from 94% paved to 55%.

17.0 Vega de Valcarce A H 🍴 🛒 ➕ 🏧, 📶 in bakery/café
1. **A** Municipal (📞72, €10): ⭐ W D 📶, Pandelo, ☎606792791, basic
2. **A** El Paso (📞28, €13): ⭐ W D 📶, Crta N-VI 6, ☎628104309, ⏰ a.y., call in winter
3. **H** Fernández (€23-29/30-41): ⭐ W D 📶, Pl Ayuntamiento 3, ☎987543027, ⏰ all year
4. **H** Las Rocas (€39/49): 🍴, Crta Antigua N-VI 53, ☎987543208
5. **H** El Recanto (€57/65): 📶, N-VI 83, ☎987543202

19.1 Ruitelán A 🍴
A Pequeño Potala (📞34, €25 🥣): 🍴 W D ⓘ, A Coruña 22, ☎987561322, ⏰ all year, Buddhist vibe, massage, vegetarian dinner

20.5 Herrerías A H 🍴
A Albergue Herrerías (📞17, €8): 🍴 W D, ☎654353940, ⏰ mid Apr-Oct, vegetarian
A H Casa Lixa (📞30, €15/-/54): 🍴 W D 📶, Camino de Santiago 35, ☎608528715
H Paraíso Bierzo (€43/56): 🍴 📶, ☎987684138
H Casa Polín (€40-50): 🍴 📶, Camino de Santiago 6, ☎987543039
H Casa Do Ferreiro (€50/56): 🍴 📶, Camino de Santiago 41, ☎987684903
H La Pandela (€48/58): 📶, Camino de Santiago 39A, ☎987199317

23.7 La Faba A 🍴 🛒
A ⭐ Albergue de la Faba (asoc, 📞52, €8 🥣): ⭐ W D ⓘ, ☎630836865, ⏰ 2pm mid Mar-Oct, evening ecumenical service, German Association

Pilgrim statue outside of La Faba albergue

Alternate: Camino Duro, 25.3km, ▲836M / ▼485M

The alternate Camino Duro route turns to the R uphill before the bridge leaving Villafranca (see photo on p. 68) and climbs a mountain, while the primary route stays in the valley.

*From the split, the path becomes a dirt path, which is initially very steep with nice views back to Villafranca. The track flattens out with lovely views and joins a paved road to the edge of **Pradela (8.9km)**. At the T turn L to continue on the trail or R to enter the Pradela. The path descends steeply on and off the paved road to **Trabadelo (11.6km)** (walk the road for a more gradual but longer descent), where the two routes join.*

8.9	**Pradela** A H 🍴
A H	Albergue Lamas (🛏10, €10/30/48): 📶 🌐 📶, Calella, ☎677569764 📧, ⊙Mar-Nov

Mountain scenery and earthen paths on the alternate route via Pradela

26 LA FABA TO TRIACASTELA

25.5km (15.8mi), ▲ **626m** / ▼ **843m**, ⏱ **6-8 Hours**
🅿 17%, 4.3km, 🆄 83%, 21.2km, **Difficulty:** ■ ■ ■

💡 The challenging climb to O Cebreiro is well rewarded with breathtaking mountain views. Traditional Galician villages provide frequent amenities and whimsical country scenery. Be prepared for cold, wet, or foggy weather. The descent to Triacastela is quite steep and can be muddy and slippery.

2.7 Laguna de Castilla A H 🍴
A H A Escuela (🛏30, €10/25/40): 🍴 W D 🅿 📶, ☎987684786, ⏱12pm Mar-Oct

5.0 O Cebreiro A H 🍴 🛒 ℹ 🚌
A Do Cebreiro (Xunta, 🛏104, €10): 🅺 W D, ☎660396809, ⏱1pm all year, no cookware
A H Casa Campelo (🛏10, €15/-/55): W D 📶 📶, O Cebreiro 9, ☎679678458 ✉, ⏱a.y.
H Hotel O Cebreiro (€40-45/50-60): 🍴, O Cebreiro 10, ☎982367182
H Casa Carolo (€46/56): Cebreiro 20, ☎982367168
H Casa Rural Navarro (€40/50): 🍴, ☎982367007 ✉
H Albergueria Frade (€40-50): O Cebreiro 21, ☎667553006

8.0 Liñares A H 🍴
A Linar do Rei (🛏20, €12/35/45): 🅼 W D 📶, ☎616464831 ✉, ⏱Mar-Nov
H Casa Jaime (€40/45): 🍴, Liñares 2, ☎982367166, all of hamlet's services here

10.5 Hospital de la Condesa A H 🍴
A Xunta (🛏20, €10): 🅺 W, ☎660396810, ⏱1pm all year, no cookware
H Mesón O Tear (€50-60): 🍴, Hospital da Condesa 14, ☎629201330

13.4 Alto do Poio A H 🍴
A H El Puerto (🛏16, €8/-/25-30): 🍴, ☎982367172
H Santa María do Poio (€40/45): Alto do Poio, ☎982367096 ✉

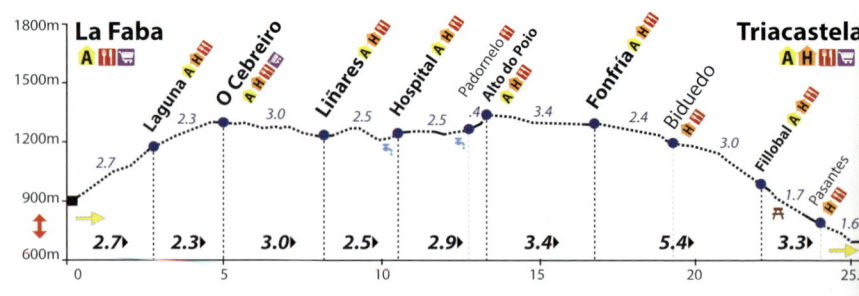

16.8 Fonfría A H ⓘ

- **A H** A Reboleira (⛺64, €13/45/50): 🍴 W D 📶 ⓘ, Camino de Santiago 15, ☎982181271, ⊙Mar-Nov
- **H** Casa de Lucas (€40/50): 🍴 📶, Fonfría 25, ☎690346740
- **H** Núñez (€45/50): 📶, Fonfría 15, ☎982161335
- **H** Casa Galego (€50/55): 📶, Fonfría 9, ☎627474783

19.2 Biduedo H ⓘ

- **H** Casa Quiroga (€45): 🍴 📶, ☎982187299
- **H** Casa Xato: (€30), ☎982187301

22.2 Fillobal A H

- **A H** Fillobal (⛺18, €13/40/47): 🐾 W D 📶, Fillobal 2, ☎666826414, ⊙all year

25.7 Triacastela

Triacastela was founded in the 9th century by Count Gatón, who was entrusted with repopulating the Bierzo region after the Reconquista. The three castles for which the town is named were built in the early 10th century and apparently destroyed in the same century with nothing remaining today, save the image on the coat of arms of Triacastela. The town held some political clout in the 13th century when Alfonxo IX spent time there and raised money for his successful bid to reconquer Sevilla.

In the *Codex Calixtinus*, Triacastela marked the end of stage 11 and signaled the end of the Galician mountains (though there are still a few smaller ups and downs to go before Santiago). The area is rich in limestone, and medieval pilgrims would often carry a large stone 100km to the limekiln in Castañeda near Santiago to be used in the making of the cathedral. Imagine the many hands that helped to build! (And be grateful you don't need to add any rocks to your pack in this day and age.)

The **Iglesia de Santiago** is mostly from the 18th century—note the three castles on the coat of arms on the tower. Evening pilgrim Mass is offered here by a particularly passionate priest. Several cafés along the main street have pilgrim *menús*.

Iglesia Santiago in Triacastela

25.5 Triacastela A H 🍴🛒➕€🚌

1. **A Xunta** (⛺56, €10): W D, ☎982548087, ⊙1pm all year, rooms of 4 and green lawn
2. **A H García** (€12/-/34-49): Peregrino 8, ☎982548024
3. **A H Lemos** (⛺12, €12/45/55): ⓚ W D 📶, Castilla 24, ☎677117238, ⊙all year
4. **A Del Oribio** (⛺27, €10): ⓚ W D, Castilla 20, ☎982548085, ⊙all year
5. **A H Atrio** (⛺20, €12/40/50): 🍴ⓚ W D 📶, Peregrino 1, ☎982548488, ⊙Feb-Nov
6. **A H A Horta de Abel** (⛺14, €11/35/40): ⓚ W D, ☎608080556, ⊙Apr-Oct
7. **A H Complexo Xacobeo** (⛺36, €12/46/56): 🍴ⓚ W D 📶◎, Leoncio Cadórnigo 12, ☎982548037, ⊙all year
8. **A Aitzenea** (⛺44, €11): ⓚ W D, Vista Alegre 1, ☎982548076, ⊙Apr-Oct
9. **A Berce Caminho** (⛺27, €11): ⓚ W D 📶, Camilo José Cela 11, ☎982548127
10. **H Casa Simón** (€55): W D 📶◎, Pl de la Iglesia 3, ☎982548438
11. **H Casa Olga** (€38/46): ⓚ W D 📶◎, Rúa do Castro, ☎982548134
12. **H Casa David** (€44/50): 🍴W D 📶, Camilo José Cela 8, ☎982548144
13. **H Vilasante** (€40/50): Camilo José Cela 7, ☎982548116

Enjoying the rainbow at the Xunta albergue in Triacastela

⛪ **Triacastela**
July 16: Virxe de Carme
Aug 17: San Mamede

Elías Valiña Sampedro bust in O Cebreiro

27

TRIACASTELA TO BARBADELO

22.5km (14.0mi), ▲ 468M / ▼ 594M, ⏱ 5-6 Hours
San Xil Route: P 47%, 10.6km, U 53%, 11.9km, **Difficulty:** 🟧🟧⬜

💡 Two options lead to Sarria/Barbadelo; both follow a mix of paved and unpaved path and have pleasing rural scenery. The most direct primary route via San Xil is 7.8km shorter (22.5km), passing through small hamlets. The longer route (30.3km) passes the Samos monastery, a fascinating historical site that includes a pilgrim albergue. The Samos route features some beautiful countryside, but the overall route has about the same distance on pavement as the San Xil route (though a lower overall %). Both routes are lovely!

2.4 A Balsa A
A El Beso (⛺12, €13): 🍴 W D, ☎633550558, ⏱all year, communal dinner from the garden

11.5 Pintín
H Casa Cines: (€45-55), Lugar Pintín 5, ☎982167939

13.4 Calvor
⚠ **A** Xunta (⛺22, €10): W D, ☎660396812, ⏱1pm all year, basic, no cookware, **Temporarily closed**

18.2 Sarria
Peregrinoteca, Benigno Quiroga 16, ☎982530190, many new pilgrims join in Sarria
1. **A** Xunta (⛺40, €10): W D, Maior 79, ☎660396813, ⏱1pm all year, fills up early with groups starting the Camino, no cookware, credenciales available
2. **A H** A Pedra (⛺15, €45-55): W D 📶, Vigo de Sarria 19, ☎982530130, ⏱Mar-Oct
3. **A** Credencial (⛺28, €12-13): 🍴 W D 📶, Peregrino 50, ☎982876455, ⏱all year
4. **A** Barullo (⛺14, €12-13/22/38): 🍴 W 📶, Plaza de Galicia 40, ☎982876357
5. **A** Oasis (⛺27, €12): W D 📶, Camino a Triacastela 12, ☎982535516, ⏱Mar-Oct
6. **A H** Alma do Camiño (⛺100, €15/35/40): W D 📶, Calvo Sotelo 199, ☎982876768, ⏱Mar-Oct

Continued on p. 76

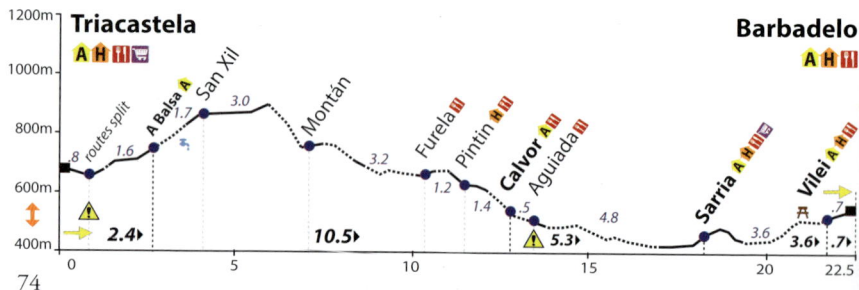

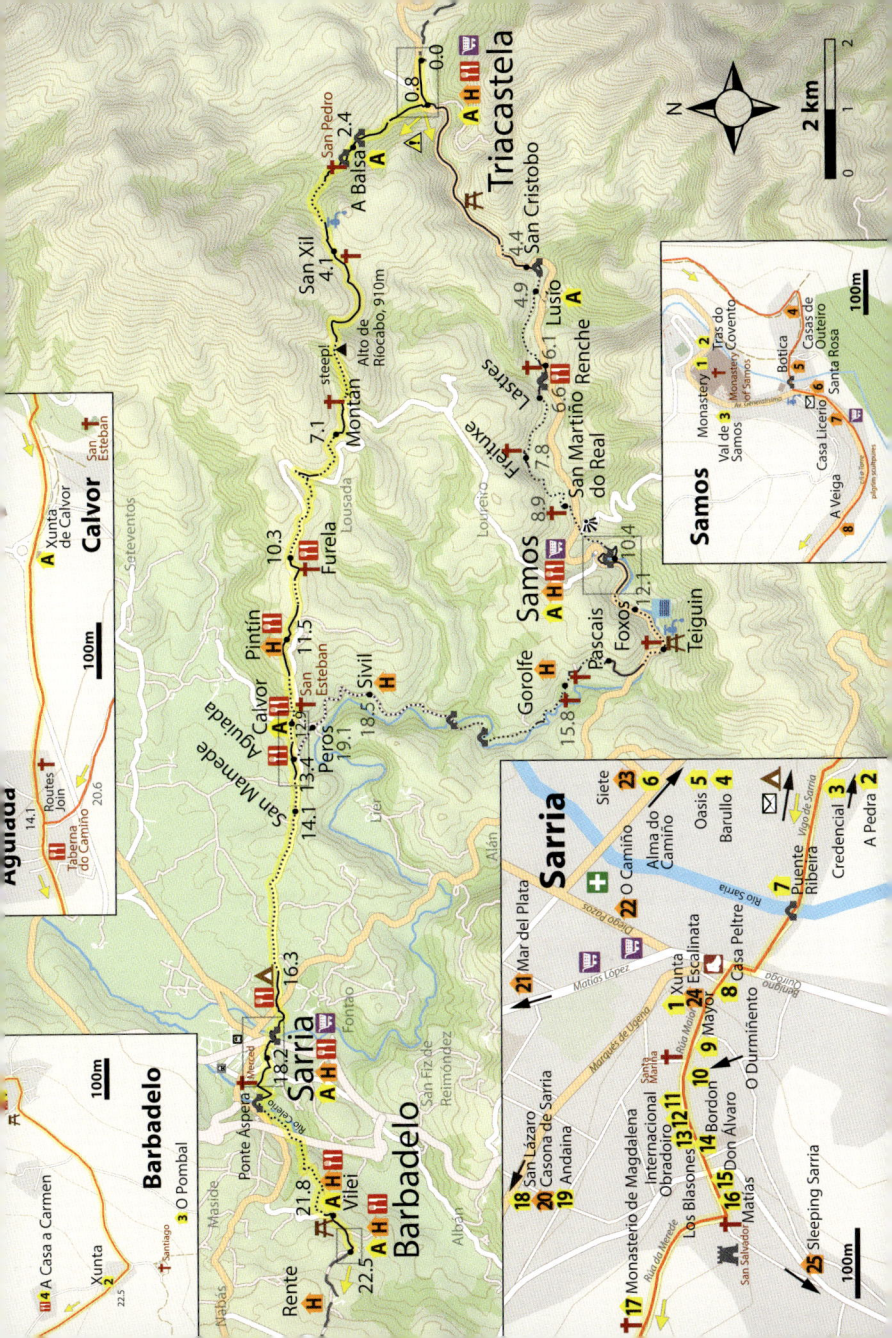

CAMINO DE SANTIAGO: CAMINO FRANCÉS

7. **A H** Puente Ribeira (⟵28, €12/-/55) 🛌Ⓦ🅳 📶, Peregrino 23, ☎982876789 📇, 🕒Mar-Oct
8. **A** Casa Peltre (⟵22, €13-14): 🛌Ⓦ🅳 📶, Escalinata Maior 10, ☎606226067 📇, 🕒Mar-Oct
9. **A** Mayor (⟵16, €13-14): 🛌Ⓦ🅳 📶, Maior 64, ☎685148474, 🕒Apr-Nov
10. **A** O Durmiñento (⟵40, €12): 🍴Ⓦ🅳 📶, Maior 44, ☎600862508, 🕒Mar-Dec
11. **A H** Internacional (⟵44, €10/30/50): 🍴Ⓦ🅳 📶, Maior 57, ☎982535109, 🕒all year
12. **A** Obradoiro (⟵38, €11-13): 🛌Ⓦ🅳 📶, Maior 49, ☎982532442, 🕒Apr-Oct
13. **A** Los Blasones (⟵42, €12): 🛌Ⓦ🅳 📶⊙, Maior 31, ☎600512565 📇, 🕒Mar-Nov
14. **A H** El Bordon de la Casa Batallon (⟵7, €12/person): 🍴🛌Ⓦ🅳 📶, Maior 29, ☎982530652 📇
15. **A H** Don Álvaro (⟵40, €15/45/60): 🛌Ⓦ🅳 📶, Maior 10, ☎982531592 📇, 🕒all year
16. **A H** Matías (⟵30, €12/40/45): 🍴Ⓦ🅳 📶, Maior 4, ☎982534285, 🕒mid Mar-Nov
17. **A** ⭐ Monasterio de Magdalena (par, ⟵100, €12): 🛌Ⓦ🅳, Merced 60, ☎982533568 📇, 🕒mid Mar-Oct, historical building
18. **A H** San Lázaro (⟵28, €12/30/40): 🛌Ⓦ🅳 📶⊙, San Lázaro 7, ☎659185482 📇, 🕒Apr-Oct
19. **A** Andaina (⟵26, €15): 🛌Ⓦ🅳 📶, Calvo Sotelo 11, ☎628232103 📇
20. **H** Casona de Sarria (€50/72): 🍴Ⓦ🅳 📶, San Lázaro 24, ☎982535556 📇, 🕒all year
21. **H** Mar del Plata (€52/61): 🍴📶, Formigueiros 5, ☎982530724 📇
22. **H** O Camiño (€30/40): 🛌📶, Benigno Quiroga 16, ☎626205172 📇
23. **H** Siete en el Camino (€40/50): 🍴🛌📶, Camiño de Pintín 10, ☎982044208 📇
24. **H** Escalinata (€40/50): Ⓦ📶, Mayor 76, ☎982530259 📇
25. **H** Sleeping Sarria (€45/50): 🛌Ⓦ🅳 📶, Esqueiredos 1, ☎689319941 📇
▲ Vila de Sarria (cabin €25): 🍴Ⓦ📶, ☎982535467 📇, 🕒Apr-Oct, 1km before town
💡 *Many more lodging options available.*

22.5 Barbadelo/Vilei **A H** 🍴 ▲

1. **A H** Casa Barbadelo (⟵48, €16/-/64): 🍴Ⓦ🅳 📶🛏, km 108, ☎982531934 📇, 🕒Apr-Oct, good reports
2. **A** Xunta (⟵18, €10): 🛌Ⓦ🅳, ☎660396814, 🕒all year
3. **A** O Pombal (⟵12, €15): 🛌Ⓦ🅳 📶, ☎686718732 📇, 🕒Apr-Oct
4. **A** Casa Carmen (⟵28, €15): 🍴📶⊙, Barbadelo 3, ☎982532294, 🕒Apr-Oct

Samos monastery

⚠ Alternate Stage 27A: Samos Route 🟫🟧
Triacastela to Barbadelo (via Samos), 30.3km, ▲467M / ▼593M
🅿 35%, 10.7km, 🆄 65%, 19.6km

4.9 Lusío 🅰
- 🅰 **Xunta** (☞60, €10): 🅺, ☎659721324, ⏱all year, bring food or be prepared to walk 1km to Renche restaurant, beautiful restored monastery, +400m

10.4 Samos 🅰🅷🍴☕➕€ℹ🚌
1. 🅰 **Monastery** (par, ☞70, don): ☎982546046 📝, basic, ⏱a.y., vespers 7:30pm
2. 🅰🅷 **Tras do Convento** (☞10, €15/-/40): 🍴🆆🅳 📶, El Salvador 1, ☎982546051 📝
3. 🅰 **Val de Samos** (☞48, €15-18): 🅺🆆🅳 📶, Comp. 16, ☎982546163 📝, ⏱Apr-Oct
4. 🅷 **Casas de Outeiro** (€66-121): 🅺 📶, Fontao 13, ☎680379969 📝, spa
5. 🅷 **A Casa da Botica** (€55/75): 🍴 📶, Fontao 2, ☎982546095 📝
6. 🅷 **Santa Rosa** (€27-45): 🅺 📶, Colledeiro 5, ☎633430219 📝
7. 🅷 **Casa Licerio** (€45/55): 🆆 📶, Comp. 44, ☎692022323 📝, by American pilgrim
8. 🅷 **Hotel A Veiga** (€45/55): 🍴🆆 📶, Compostela 61, ☎982546052 📝

15.8 Gorolfe
- 🅷 **Hotel Casa Monte Oribio** (€65-95): 🍴📶🛏, Vilachá 4, ☎613326603 📝

18.5 Sivil 🅷
- 🅷 **A Fonte das Bodas** (€45-55): 📶, ☎637138636 📝

28

BARBADELO TO HOSPITAL ALTA DA CRUZ

29.9km (18.6mi), ▲ 630M / ▼ 510M, ⏱ 6-7.5 Hours
🅿 40%, 12.0km, Ⓤ 60%, 17.9km, **Difficulty:** ▬▬▢

💡 Today's route climbs to the Alto de Páramo, dips down to the riverside town of Portomarín, and ascends again toward the Sierra Ligonde. The path passes almost constantly through small nearly-abandoned hamlets. Many villages and towns offer intermediate accommodations, including Portomarín with many albergues and the last grocery shop until Palas de Rei in the next stage.

1.0 Rente H Casa Nova de Rente (€30/40): ☎982187854 📝

1.7 Serra A H 🛒
⚠ A Molino Marzán (🛏16, €12): 🍴 W D 📶, ☎679438077 📝, 🕐Mar-Oct, 1.4km past Serra, **Temporarily closed**

7.7 Morgade A H 🍴
A H Casa Morgade (🛏6, €15/52/65): 🍴 W D, ☎982531250 📝, 🕐Easter-Oct

9.0 Ferreiros A H 🍴 🏧
A Xunta (🛏22, €10): K W D, ☎660396815, 🕐1pm all year, no cookware
A H Casa Cruceiro (🛏24, €14/-/55): 🍴 W D 📶, ☎982541240 📝, 🕐Apr-Nov

9.9 Pena A H 🍴
A H Casa do Rego (🛏6, €15/-/60: 🍴 W D 📶 Ⓞ, A Pena 4, ☎711717913 📝

12.6 Mercadoiro A H 🍴
A H Mercadoiro (🛏22, €12/-/60-85): 🍴 W D 📶, Aldea Mercadoiro 2, ☎982545359 📝, 🕐Mar-Nov 15

15.7 Vilachá A H 🍴
⚠ A H ⛺ Casa Banderas (🛏8, €14/40/45): 🍴 W D 📶 Ⓞ, As Cortes 5, 682179589 📝, 🕐Apr-Oct, camping, run by California family, **Temporarily closed**

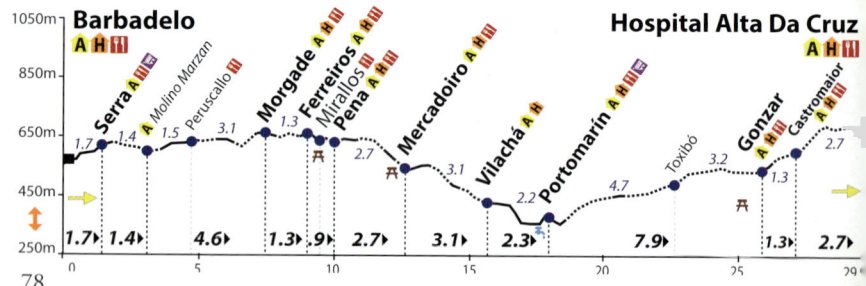

18.0 Portomarín A H 🛒➕ℹ️🚌

1. **A** Xunta (🛏110, €10): 🅺🆆🅳, Fraga Iribarne, ☎982545143, ⏰1pm a.y., crowded
2. **A H** Albergue Manuel (🛏16, €14/30/37): 🅺🆆🅳⭕, do Miño 1, ☎679754718
3. **A H** Pons Minea (🛏24, €15/50/60): 🍴, Sarria 11, ☎610737995, ⏰Apr-Oct, poor reports
4. **A H** Casa Marabillas (🛏16, €16/30/45): 🅺🆆🅳📶, ☎744450425, ⏰Mar-Oct
5. **A H** PortoSantiago (🛏14, €15/55/65): 🅺🆆🅳📶⭕, Diputación 8, ☎618826515
6. **A H** Ultreia (🛏15, €15/55/60): 🅺🆆🅳📶⭕, Diputación 9, ☎982545067
7. **A H** El Caminante (🛏12, €12/30/45): 🍴🆆🅳📶, ☎982545176, ⏰Apr-Oct
8. **A** Novo Porto (🛏22, €12): 🅺🆆🅳📶, B. Quiroga 12, ☎982545277, ⏰Apr-Oct
9. **A** Casa Cruz (🛏16, €12): 🍴🅺🆆🅳, Benigno Quiroga 16, ☎982545140, ⏰all year
10. **A** Villamartín (🛏22, €12): 🅺🆆🅳📶, ☎982545054, ⏰Apr-Oct, poor reports
11. **A H** Huellas (🛏6, €18/-/50): 🅺🆆🅳📶, do Peregrino 15, ☎681398278
12. **A** Pasiño a Pasiño (🛏30, €14): 🅺🆆🅳📶⭕, Compostela 25, ☎665667243
13. **A H** Casona da Ponte (🛏47, €15/-/80): 🍴🅺🆆🅳📶⭕, ☎982169862
14. **A** Ferramenteiro (🛏130, €14): 🍴🅺🆆🅳📶⭕, ☎982545362, ⏰Mar-Oct
15. **A H** Aqua Portomarín (🛏10, €12/45/50): 🅺🆆🅳📶, ☎608921372, ⏰Mar-Nov
16. **A** Folgueira (🛏32, €14): 🅺🆆🅳📶, Chantada 18, ☎982545166, ⏰all year
17. **H** Portomiño (€50-60): 🍴📶, Sarria 2, ☎982547575
18. **H** Casa do Maestro (€60/75): 🅺📶🛏, Fraga Iribarne 1, ☎982545318
19. **H** Pousada de Portomarín (€68-75): 🍴📶🛏, Sarria, ☎982545200

17.7 Portomarín has been around for a while with a bridge from at least the late 10th century, but the current city is a relocation of the historic city including buildings transferred stone by stone. This was all due to a dam constructed in 1956, which flooded the former city that was located on both sides of the river. Today the water is normally low enough to see the remnants of the former city including the Roman bridge. Many bridges have spanned the river at this strategic point. Al-Mansur destroyed an early bridge in his campaign of devastation in 997. After being rebuilt, the bridge was taken out again by the 1112 war between Queen Urraca and her husband. Later, Urraca had the bridge rebuilt along with a pilgrim hospital. The strategic town needed to be protected, and this role fell first to the Order of Santiago, then to the Order of San Juan de Jerusalén.

Remains of the former Portomarín now flooded by the Río Miño

The town became an important pilgrim stopping point, including for royal pilgrims such as King Ferdinand and Queen Isabella. Domenico Laffi described it as, "an excellent place that has plenty of everything." The city declined in the 19th century as the nearby city of Lugo rose to prominence.

At the top of the staircase entering town is the relocated **Capela da Virxe das Neves**, a chapel with an image of the virgin traditionally thought to protect from drowning. The main church in town is the **Iglesia de San Nicolás** with its fortress-like appearance and prominent rose window. The portal was crafted by Master Mateo, a famous architect who also built the *Pórtico de Gloria* in the Santiago Cathedral. The church was transported brick by brick from its old location.

25.9 Gonzar A H

A Xunta (28, €10): on the highway, 982157840, 1pm all year
A H Casa García (26, €12/-/40): 982157842, Mar-Oct, good reports
A H Albergue-Hostería de Gonzar (20, €12/45/55): Gonzar 7, 982154878, Easter-Nov

27.2 Castromaior A H

A H Ortiz (18, €14/30/50): Castromaior 2, 982099416, poor reports
H Casa Perdigueira (€45-60): Castromaior 9, 690852026

29.9 Hospital Alta da Cruz A H

1. **A Xunta** (32, €10): along highway, 982545232, 1pm all year
2. **H Hostal Labrador** (€45/50): Alto Hospital 2, 982545303

Iglesia de San Juan/Nicolás in Portomarín (left)

29 HOSPITAL ALTA DA CRUZ TO MELIDE

28.1km (17.5mi), ▲ 418M / ▼ 644M, ⏱ 7-8 Hours
P 25%, 7.0km, U 75%, 21.1km, **Difficulty:** ▬▬▬

☀ This stage traverses rolling hills, alternating between dirt tracks and quiet country lanes. Small villages offer frequent services with many intermediate accommodations options. Leave Lugo province behind and enter **A Coruña**, now firmly in the seafood zone where octopus is the claim to fame.

1.5 Ventas de Narón A H ¶

A H O Cruceiro (⌂22, €15/-/40): Ventas 6, ☎658064917, ✉, ⏱Mar-Oct
A H Casa Molar (⌂18, €12/-/35): Ventas 4, ☎696794507, ✉, ⏱Mar-Oct

5.1 Ligonde A H ¶

A Fuente del Peregrino (par, ⌂7, don): Ligonde 4, ☎687550527, ✉, ⏱May-Oct, communal meals, run by Christian association
H Casa Tania (€38-60): Ligonde 28, ☎604047316 ✉

5.7 Eirexe A H ¶

A △ Xunta (⌂20, €10): Airexe 7, ☎982153483, ⏱1pm all year, no cookware
A H Eirexe (⌂6, €10/25/40): Airexe 18, ☎982153475, ⏱Easter-Oct

7.7 Portos A H ¶

A H A Paso de Formiga (⌂8, €14/50/70): Portos 4, ☎618984605 ✉

12.3 Os Chacotes A H ¶ (recreation area 1km before Palas de Rei)

A Os Chacotes (Xunta, ⌂112, €10): As Lagartas, ☎607481536, ⏱all year, no cookware
H Alda (€87-123): Doctor Pardo Ouro, ☎982380750 ✉

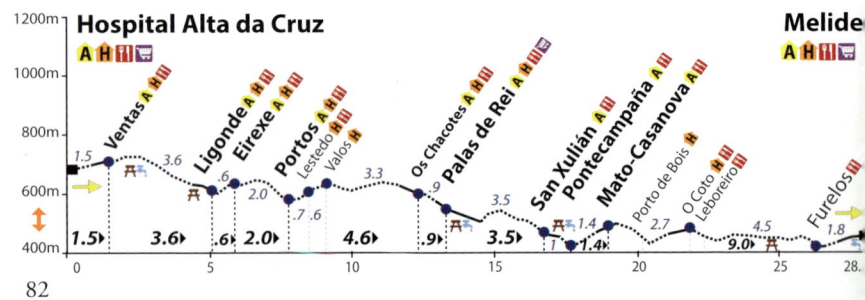

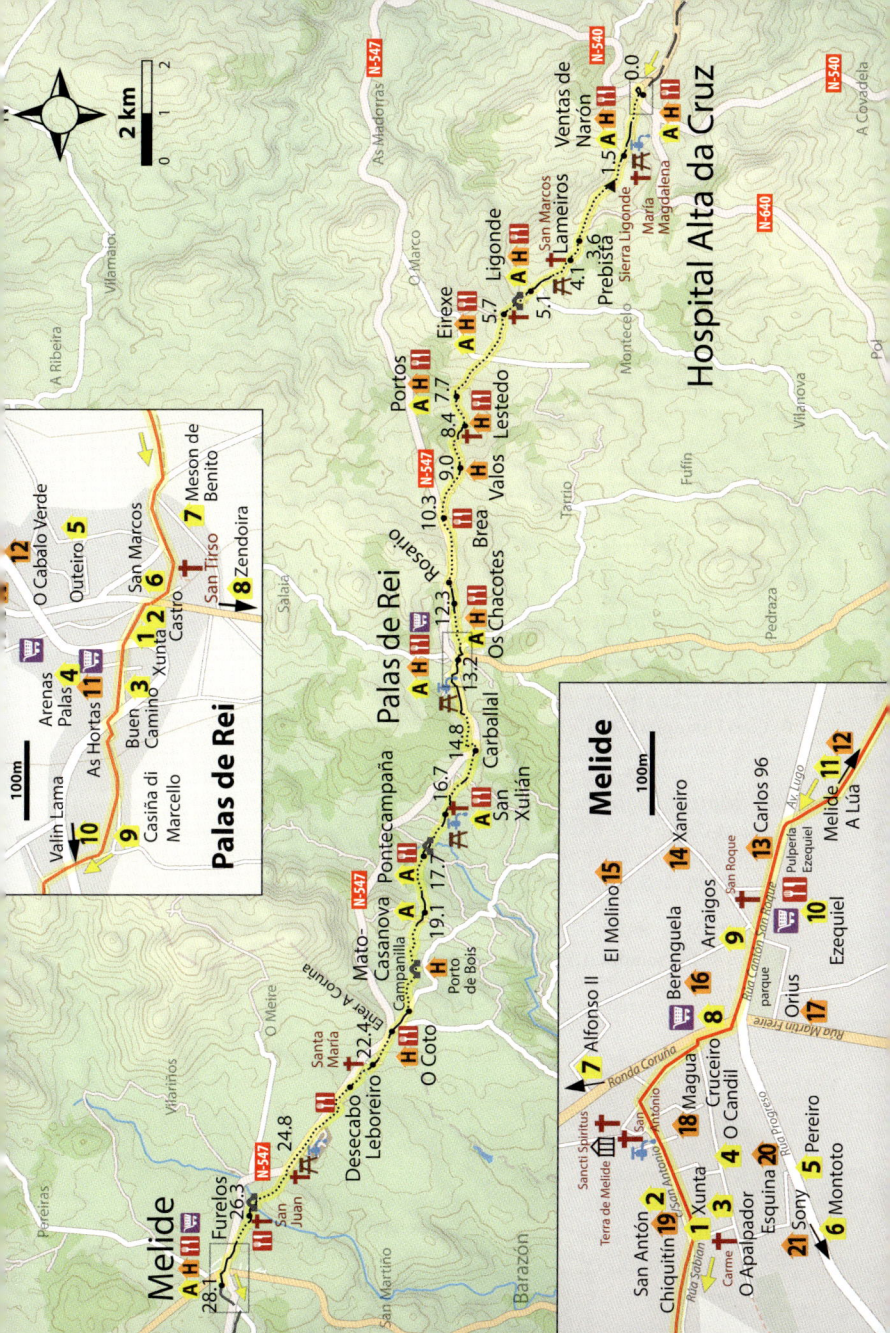

CAMINO DE SANTIAGO: CAMINO FRANCÉS

13.2 Palas de Rei
1. **Xunta** (⚯60, €10): Compostela 19, ☎660396820, ⌚1pm a.y., downtown
2. **Castro** (⚯56, €14): Ourense 24, ☎609080655, ⌚all year
3. **Buen Camino** (⚯42, €14): Peregrino 3, ☎982380233, ⌚Mar 15 - Oct 15
4. **Arenas Palas** (⚯26, €14/36/50): Compostela 16, ☎982380326
5. **Outeiro** (⚯50, €13): Pl Galicia 25, ☎982380242, ⌚Mar-Oct
6. **San Marcos** (⚯72, €18/-/65): Travesía Iglesia, ☎982380711, ⌚Mar-Oct
7. **Mesón de Benito** (⚯100, €14): Da Paz, ☎636834065, ⌚Apr-Oct
8. **Zendoira** (⚯28, €17/-/60): Amado Losada 10, ☎608-490075, ⌚Mar-Oct, bed pods w/curtain, bike workshop
9. **Casiña di Marcello** (⚯17, €16-20/-/55-65): Aldeia de Abaixo 13, ☎640723903, ⌚Apr-mid Nov, shared dinner
10. **Valin Lama** (⚯30, €16): Av. Compostela 58, ☎646479235
11. **As Hortas** (€59/79): das Hortas 7, ☎626518388
12. **O Cabalo Verde** (€45): Travesía do Mercado 2, ☎679911186
13. **Pensión Palas** (€40-70): San Tirso, ☎982380065

16.7 San Xulián
O Abrigadoiro (⚯18, €15): ☎676596975

17.7 Pontecampaña
Casa Domingo (⚯21, €15): ☎630728864, ⌚Easter-Oct, communal dinner

19.1 Mato-Casanova
Xunta (⚯20, €10): ☎982173483, ⌚1pm all year, no cookware
A Bolboreta (€62/71): Vilar de Remonde, ☎609-124717, ⌚all year, offer pickup, 1.2km past Mato-Casanova, +200m

21.8 O Coto
Casa de los Somoza (€60-88): ☎605883268
Pensión Baires (€34/38): ☎645118958

Wooden *hórreos*, used for grain storage in Galicia

Octopus, a Melide specialty, at Pulpería Ezequiel

28.1 Melide A H 🛒 ➕ € 🛈 🏧

1. **A Xunta** (📞156, €10): 🇰🇼🇩🚌, San Antonio, 📞660396822, 🕐1pm a.y., no cookware
2. **A San Antón** (📞36, €16): 🍴🇰🇼🇩📶, San Antonio 6, 📞981506427 📧, 🕐Mar-Oct
3. **A O Apalpador** (📞30, €14): 🇰🇼🇩📶, San Antonio 23, 📞679837969 📧, 🕐all year
4. **H A O Candil** (€18/-/50 🛍): 🍴🇰🇼🇩📶🅾, Principal 21, 📞639503550 📧, 🕐12pm Mar-Oct
5. **A Pereiro** (📞45, €14): 🇰🇼🇩📶🅾, Progreso 43, 📞981506314 📧, 🕐all year
6. **A H Montoto** (📞40, €14/32/40): 🇰🇼🇩📶, Codeseira 31, 📞646941887 📧
7. **A H Alfonso II** (📞35, €17-19/-/55): 🇼🇩📶🅾, Ac. Toques e Friol 52, 📞981506454
8. **A O Cruceiro** (📞72, €13): 🇼🇩📶, Ronda Coruña 2, 📞616764896 📧, 🕐Mar-Oct
9. **A Arraigos** (📞20, €13): 🇼🇩📶, Cantón S. Roque 9, 📞600880769 📧, 🕐all year
10. **A Ezequiel** (📞18, €16): 🍴🇼🇩, Rúa Sol 7, 📞686583378 📧, 🕐all year, restaurant known for octopus
11. **A Melide** (📞42, €15/-/34): 🇼🇩📶, Lugo 92, 📞627901552 📧, 🕐Easter-Oct, lockers
12. **H A Lúa do Camiño** (€45-65): 🇼📶🛏, Circunvalación, 📞620958331 📧
13. **H Hotel Carlos 96** (€43/63 🛍): 🍴📶, Lugo 119, 📞981507633 📧, quad rooms €80
14. **H Hotel Xaneiro** (€55): 🍴📶, Habana 43, 📞981506140 📧
15. **H El Molino** (€35-45): 🍴📶, Rosalia de Castro 23, 📞981506048 📧
16. **H Pensión Berenguela** (€39/59): 📶, San Roque 2, 📞981505417 📧
17. **H Pensión Orois** (€45/50): 🛍📶, Alexandre Boveda 13, 981507097 📧
18. **H Pousada Chiquitín** (€45/50): 🍴📶, San Antonio 18, 📞981815333 📧
19. **H Casa Magua** (€31/40): 📶, Camiño de Ovedo 23, 📞601640340 📧, pet friendly
20. **H Pensión Esquina** (€40/68): 🛍📶, Ichoas 1, 627570685 📧
21. **H Pensión Restaurante Sony** (€ 42/52): 🍴📶, Cedeseira, 📞981506473 📧

30 MELIDE TO ARCA

33.0km (20.5mi), ▲ 602M / ▼ 781M, ⊙ 8-10 Hours
P 30%, 9.9km, U 70%, 23.1km, **Difficulty:** ▬ ▬

💡 A long stage with constant ups and downs through small villages and the larger pilgrim town of Arzúa. There are frequent services and many overnight options. Fragrant eucalyptus groves provide plenty of shade.

5.5 Boente A H 🚌
- **A H Boente** (🛏54, €16/50/60-65): 🍴 W D 📶 🅿, ☎981501974 📩, ⊙Mar-Nov
- **A Fuente Saleta** (🛏30, €14): W D 📶, ☎981501853, ⊙all year
- **A El Alemán** (🛏40, €15): 🍴 W D 📶 ⊙ 🅿, Arriba 49, ☎981501984 📩, ⊙Mar-Oct
- **H Rectoral de Boente** (€82/102 🛍): 🍴 📶, Boente de Arriba 16, ☎684238323 📩

7.8 Castañeda A H 🚌
Castañeda was the destination of the limestone that medieval pilgrims carried from Triacastela to be finished in the ovens and used in constructing the cathedral.
- **A H Santiago** (🛏4, €13/-/40): 🍴 W D 📶, ☎981501711, ⊙call in winter
- **H Casa Rural Milia** (€82/102): 🍴 📶, Lugar Portela, ☎981501625 📩, +600m off route
- **H Casa Rural Garea** (€45/50): 🍴 📶, Lugar da Portela, ☎981500400 📩

10.8 Ribadiso da Baixo A H 🍴 🚌
The pilgrim hospital of San Antón served pilgrims in the 16th century and was restored in 1993 to return to use as a Xunta albergue.
- **A Xunta** (🛏70, €10): K W D ⊙, ☎981501185, ⊙1pm all year, no cookware, restored historic buildings along the river
- **A H ▲ Los Caminantes** (🛏56, €14/38/48): K W D 📶, ☎647020600 📩, ⊙Apr-Oct
- **A Milpés** (🛏24, €15): 🍴 ⊙ W D 📶, Ribadiso 7, ☎981500425 📩
- **A H Miraiso** (🛏10, €16/41/55): ⊙ W D 📶, Ribadiso 8, ☎634117568 📩
- **H Pensión Ribadiso** (€80): 📶 🅿, ☎669131955 📩
- **H ▲ Teiraboa Base Camp** (€42-75, ▲ €10): 🍴 W D 🅿, N-547 km 62, ☎981193102 📩

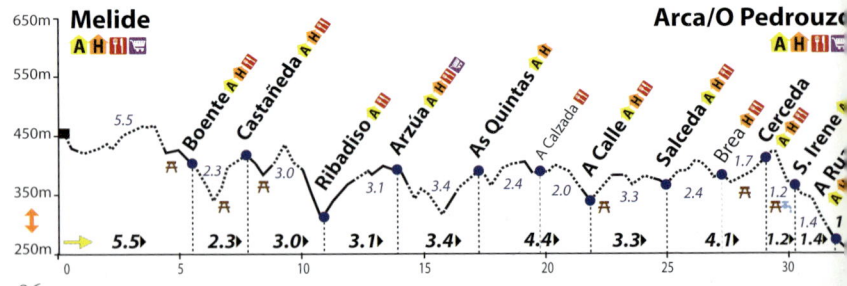

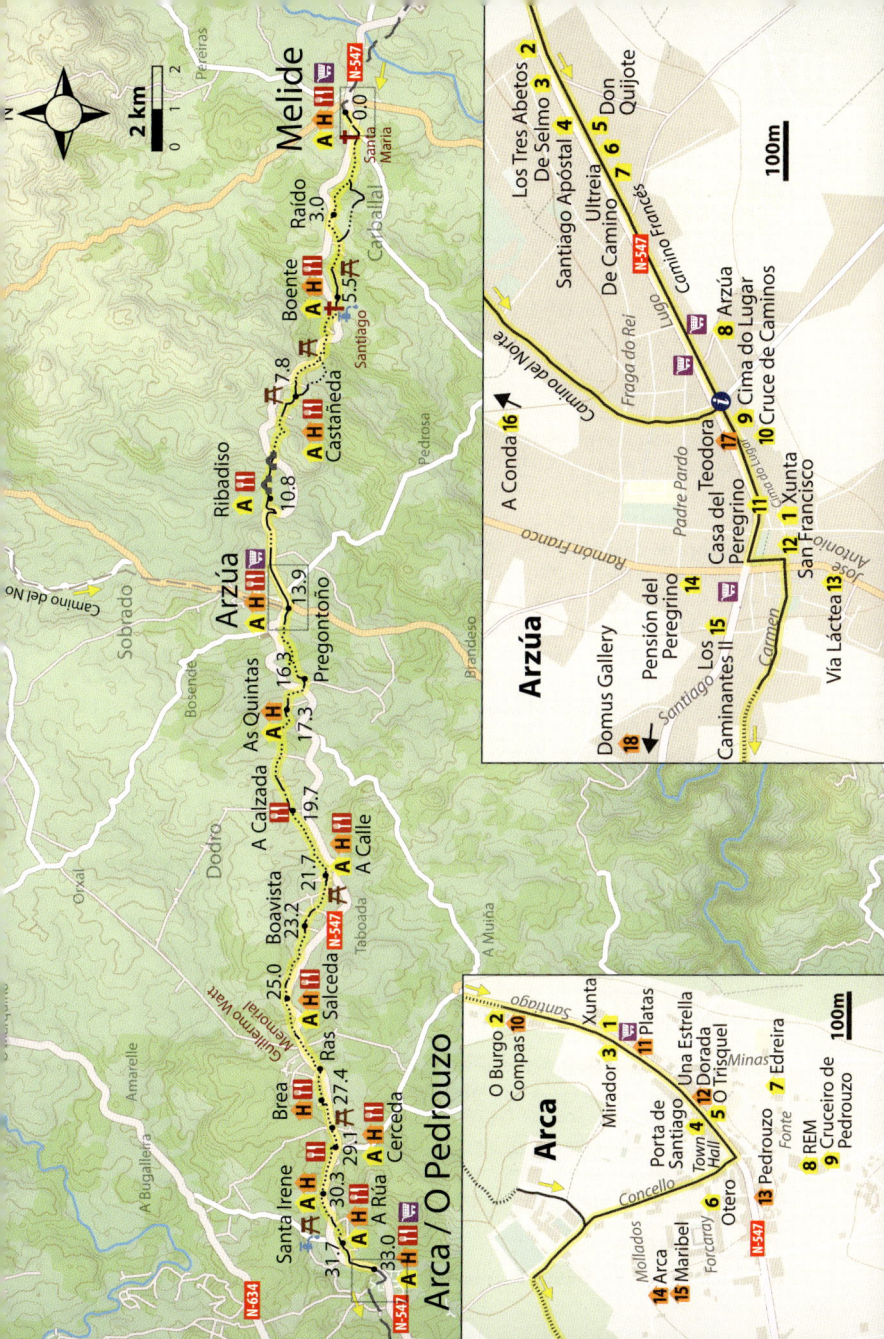

13.9 Arzúa

Arzúa was previously known as Villanova, as it is called in the Codex Calixtinus. Two pilgrim hospices were located here. The Iglesia de Santiago is a 20th-century structure with a 19th-century retablo depicting the battle of Clavijo and Santiago Matamoros' appearance. The town is famous for its delicious creamy cheese. The central plaza features a statue of a cheesemaker, and an annual March cheese festival sells over 100,000 cheeses each year. This was the traditional stopping point before Santiago for medieval pilgrims.

1. **A Xunta** (⇌48, €10): Cima de Lugar 6, ☏660396824, ⊙1pm all year
2. **A Los Tres Abetos** (⇌42, €18): Rúa Lugo, ☏649771142
3. **A De Selmo** (⇌50, €16-17): Lugo 133, ☏981939018
4. **A Santiago Apóstol** (⇌72, €12): Lugo 107, ☏981508132, ⊙all year
5. **A Don Quijote** (⇌50, €15): L.130, ☏981500139, ⊙all year
6. **A Ultreia** (⇌39, €14): Lugo 126, ☏981500471, ⊙all year
7. **A De Camino** (⇌42, €15): Lugo 118, ☏981500415, ⊙Mar-Nov
8. **A H Arzúa** (⇌12, €14/-/40-50): Rosalía Castro 2, ☏981508233, ⊙Feb-Nov
9. **A H Cima do Lugar** (⇌14, €15/48/60): Lugar 22, ☏981500559, ⊙a.y.
10. **A Cruce de Caminos** (⇌56, €17-22): Cima do Lugar 28, ☏604051353
11. **A Casa del Peregrino** (⇌14, €12): Cima do Lugar 7, ☏686708704
12. **A H San Francisco** (⇌28, €16/35/50): Carmen 7, ☏881979304
13. **A Vía Láctea** (⇌60, €17): José N. Vilas 26, ☏981500581, ⊙all year
14. **A Pensión del Peregrino** (€18/-/50-55): Ramón Franco 7, ☏981500145
15. **A Caminantes II** (⇌28, €13): Santiago 14, ☏647020600, ⊙Apr-Oct
16. **A H A Conda/Vilariño Moscoso** (€15/-/62): Calexa 92, ☏670385351, ⊙Apr-Oct
17. **H Teodora** (€70): ☏981500083
18. **H Domus Gallery** (€49/71): Santiago 61, ☏628873791

17.3 As Quintas

A △ Taberna Vella - Heidi's Place (⇌8, €17): ☏687543810, ⊙Apr-Oct
A H Camiño das Ocas (⇌30, €13/-/50-60): ☏648404780, +800m

21.7 A Calle

A Ponte de Ferreiros (⇌30, €15): ☏665641877, ⊙all year, +200m
H Mirador de Rouris (€40/50-60): Rouris 9, ☏608981630
H Casa do Horreo (€89-95): A Calle 6, ☏626616758, ⊙Apr-Nov

25.0 Salceda

A H Alborada (⇌10, €15/50/60): ☏981502956, ⊙Apr-Oct
A H Salceda (⇌8, €17/55/68): N547 km 75, ☏981502767, ⊙a.y., +400m
A La Corona (⇌20, €15): Salceda 22, ☏675149086
H Casa Tia Teresa (€39-45): Salceda 14, ☏628558716
H Tasaga (€60): Salceda 23, ☏981113077

27.4 Brea

H O Mesón (€35/50): A Brea 16, ☏981511040

MELIDE TO ARCA 30

29.1 Cerceda A H 🍴🚆
- **A Andaina** (🛏15, €13): 🍴 W D 📶,
  O Empalme de Santa Irene 11,
  ☏981502925
- **H O Pozo** (€67/77): O Castro 28,
  ☏676640199

30.3 Santa Irene A H 🚆
- **A Xunta** (🛏36, €10): 🅺 W D,
  ☏660396825, ⏰1pm all year,
  no cookware, restaurant nearby
- **A Santa Irene** (🛏15, €14): 🍴 W D 📶 ⊙,
  ☏981511000, ⏰Apr-Oct, charming
- **A Astrar** (🛏24, €12-14): 🅺 W D 📶, Astrar 18,
  ☏608092820 📍, ⏰Mar-Nov, +700m

Arzúa street café

31.7 A Rúa A H 🍴🚆
- **A Espíritu Santo Xacobeo** (🛏46, €16-18): 🅺 W D 📶 ⊙, ☏620635284 📍, ⏰Apr-Oct
- **A▲ Kampoah** (🛏112, €12-13): 🍴 W D 📶 🚆, A Rúa 28, ☏981197125 📍, ⏰Apr-Oct
- **H O Acivro** (€80): 🍴🚆, A Rúa 28, ☏981511316 📍
- **H O Pino** (€45-58/60-70): 🍴📶, A Rúa 9, ☏981511035 📍

33.0 Arca A H 🍴🚆🛒➕⊙ℹ🚆 Also O Pino or O Pedrouzo, ℹ ☏981511065, At the entrance to Arca, turn L to enter town for accommodations or services, or continue straight to bypass Arca, passing one café on the far side of town (saves 0.6km). Arca once housed the Hospital de Santa Eulalia de Arca and the Capilla de San Antón de Arca, though nothing remains of them today. There is a modern Iglesia de Santa Eulalia de Arca and impressive oak trees near town hall.

1. **A Xunta** (🛏120, €10): 🅺 W D, Lugo 30, ☏660396826, ⏰1pm a.y., near post office
2. **A H O Burgo** (🛏10, €45-58/60-70): W D 📶 ⊙, L. 47, ☏630404138 📍, ⏰Apr-Oct
3. **A Mirador de Pedrouzo** (🛏50, €14-16): 🍴 W D 📶 ⊙, ☏686871215 📍, ⏰all year
4. **A Porta de Santiago** (🛏54, €12): 🅺 W D 📶 ⊙, L. 11, ☏981511103 📍, ⏰Mar-N
5. **A O Trisquel** (🛏68, €14): 🅺 W D 📶, Picón 1, ☏616644740 📍
6. **A Otero** (🛏36, €14): 🅺 W D, Forcarei 2, ☏671663374 📍, ⏰Ap-Oct
7. **A Edreira** (🛏56, €13): 🅺 W D 📶 ⊙, ☏981511365 📍, ⏰Mar-Oct
8. **A REM** (🛏50, €13-14): 🅺 W D 📶, Iglesia 7, ☏981510407, ⏰all year
9. **A Cruceiro de Pedrouzo** (🛏94, €12-14): 🅺 W D 📶, ☏981511371, ⏰Mar-Oct
10. **H Pensión Compas** (€30/42): 🍴📶, Lugo 47, ☏981511309 📍
11. **H Pensión Platas** (€70): 📶, Lugo 26, ☏981511378 📍
12. **H Una Estrella Dorada** (€80): 🅺 W 📶, Lugo 10, ☏630018363
13. **H Pensión Pedrouzo** (€50-60): W D 📶, Santiago 13, ☏671663375 📍
14. **H Pensión Arca** (€45/55): 🅺 📶, Mollados 25, ☏657888594 📍
15. **H Hostal Maribel** (€60/65-70): 🅺, Mollados 23, ☏981511404 📍

31

ARCA TO SANTIAGO DE COMPOSTELA

20.2km (12.6mi), ▲ 360M / ▼ 379M, ⏱ 4-5.5 Hours
🅿 63%, 12.7km, 🆄 37%, 7.5km, **Difficulty:** ▬ ▬ ▯

💡 The path today passes through eucalyptus forests and small villages to Monte do Gozo, within sight (on a clear day) of Santiago's cathedral spires. The last 5km are city walking. The atmosphere entering Santiago is often jubilant, with singing, shouting and congratulations, no matter how dreary the weather. Leave early to arrive in time for the noon pilgrim Mass.

3.7 Amenal 🄷🄷
- **H** Hotel Amenal (€71/79): 🔆, ☎981510431
- **H** Pensión Kilómetro 15 (€45/55): 🔆, Codesal 11, ☎981897086
- **H** Pensión CHE (€60): 🔆, Cimadevila 11, ☎981814367, +500m

10.0 Lavacolla A 🄷🄷🄼🄳, "place of washing"
- **A** Lavacolla (📞34, €14): 🄺🅆🔆, Lavacolla 35, ☎981897274
- **A** Fábrica (📞32, €20): 🄺🅆🄳🄾, Lavacolla 55, ☎681075647
- **H** A Concha (€43/53): 🔆, Lavacolla 1, ☎981888390
- **H** San Paio (€45/60): 🔆, Lavacolla 54, ☎981888205
- **H** Garcas (€70): 🄺🔆, Naval 2, ☎981888225
- **H** Ruta Jacobea (€99): 🔆, Lavacolla 41, ☎981888211
- **H** Pazo Xan Xordo (€ 89-105): 🔆, Xan Xordo 6, ☎981888259, +900m

14.6 San Marcos 🄷🄼🄼
- **H** Hotel Akelarre (€60): 🔆, Av. San Marcos 37, ☎981552689
- **▲** Peregrino San Marcos (camping €10): 🄺🅆🄳🔆, Lugar Lagoa 9, ☎634109331

15.3 Monte do Gozo A 🄷🄼▲🄳, Galician: *Monxoi* "Mount Joy"
- **A** Xunta (📞500, €10): 🄺🅆🄳🔆, ☎981558942, ⏱1pm all year, rooms of 8
- **A H** Albergue Monte do Gozo (📞121, €16-18/-/62-80): 🄺🅆🄳🔆, Rúa do Gozo 18, ☎981558942, same complex as Xunta albergue
- **H** Santiago Apóstal (€70-125): 🄺🅆🄳🔆, San Marcos 1, ☎981557155

20.0 Santiago de Compostela A 🄷🄼🄼🅇🄾🄸🄸🄼🅇🅇
See city map and accommodations list on p. 92-23.

Arca/O Pedrozo — A H 🄼
Santiago de Compostel — A H 🄼

San Anton 1.4, 2.3, Amenal 4.0, San Paio, 2.3, Lavacolla A H 🄼, Vilamaior, 1.3, 3.4, San Marcos H 🄼, Monte de Gozo A H, .6, 2.2, San Lázaro A H 🄼, 2.7

10.0▶ 5.3 2.2▶ 2.7▶

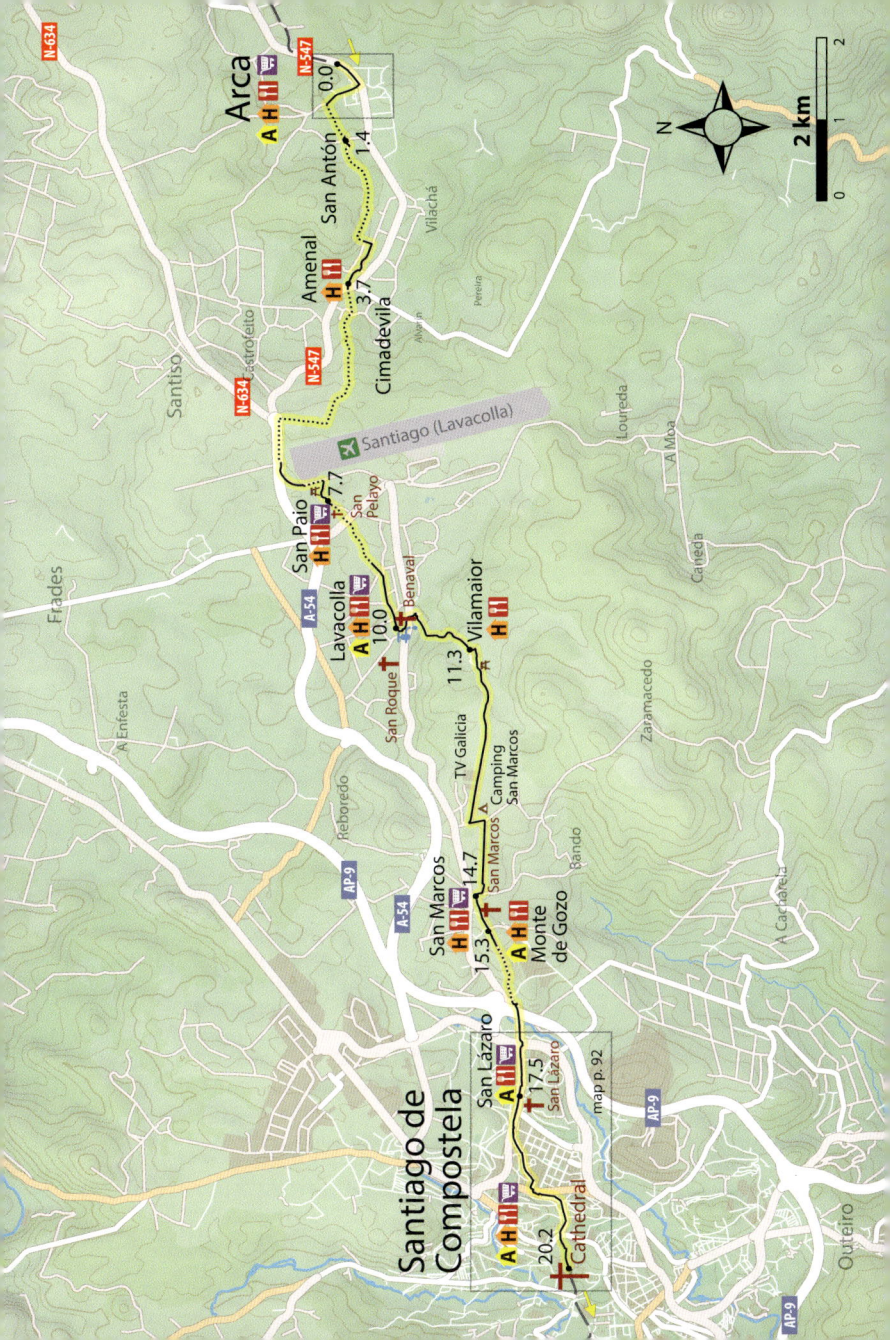

0.2 Santiago de Compostela

Pilgrim office: Rúa Carretas 33, ☎981568846, ⏱9am-7pm (except Dec 25 & Jan 1),
Santiago city: Rúa do Vilar 63, ☎981555129, ⏱Daily 10am-6pm
Galicia: Plaza Mazarelos 15, ☎881866397, ⏱M-Sa 10am-5pm (closed Sundays)

- **Sixtos** (⚐40, €22-30/-/60): Fonte Concheiros 2, ☎881067936, ⏱Mar-Nov, no 🚲
- **Santos** (⚐24, €22-25/-/60): Concheiros 48, ☎881169386, ⏱Mar-Nov
- **Estrella de Santiago** (⚐24, €13-25): Concheiros 36-38, ☎881973926, ⏱a.y.
- **Porta Real** (⚐24, €22-25): Concheiros 10, ☎633610114, ⏱a.y., no bike storage
- **Seminario Menor** (⚐177, €22-24/26-28/52-56): Quiroga Palacios 2, ☎881031768, ⏱Mar-Oct, all beds not bunks, lockers available
- **Meiga Backpackers** (hostel, ⚐30, €19-26): Basquiños 67, ☎981570846, ⏱all year
- **LoopINN** (€19-26): Tras de Santa Clara, ☎981585667
- **Fogar de Teodomiro** (hstl, ⚐20, €19-25): Algalia Arriba 3, ☎981582920
- **Linares** (⚐14, €16-23): Algalia Abajo 34, ☎981580443
- **Last Stamp** (⚐54, €20-25): Preguntoiro 10, ☎981563525, ⏱mid Jan-mid Dec
- **Azabache** (⚐20, €24-30): Azabachería 15, ☎981071254, ⏱all year
- **Santiago KM-0** (⚐41, €27-32): das Carretas 11, ☎881974992
- **Blanco** (⚐20, €25/45/55): Galeras 30, ☎881976850
- **Mundoalbergue** (⚐34, €19-22): San Clemente 26, ☎981588625, ⏱all year
- **La Estación** (⚐24, €18-20): Xoana Nogueira 14, ☎981594624, ⏱all year
- **A Casa Do Peregrino** (€100-150): Azabacheria 2, ☎981573931
- **Altaïr Hotel** (€125-150): Loureiros 12, ☎981554712
- **Costa Vella** (€78-88/97-114): Porta da Pena 17, ☎981569530, restored Jesuit house
- ⭐ **San Martín Pinario** (pilgrim €29/45): Plaza Inmaculada 3, ☎981560282, call or email for pilgrim price
- **Dos Reis Católicos** (€280-350+): Praza do Obradoiro, ☎981582200, Parador
- **Costa Azul** (€38-41/64-71): Das Galeras 18, ☎602451906
- **Pensión Fonseca** (€34/60): Fonseca 1, ☎981584145
- **Hostal Suso** (€87-98): Villar 65, ☎981586611
- **Pensión Centro** (€40/55): Senra 11, ☎981588465

CAMINO DE SANTIAGO: CAMINO FRANCÉS

20.0 Santiago de Compostela!

This magical and vibrant city has much to offer, but your first priority is likely to head to the cathedral to visit the tomb and pay your respects to the Apostle who has drawn you to this place. Daily pilgrim Mass is offered at noon. With all the affordable private accommodation in Santiago, we suggest foregoing the albergue for a modest pensión or splurging on one of the fine hotels.

Historical evidence suggests that Santiago was once a Roman city, followed by Visigothic rule. The kings of Galicia and León were crowned here at the cathedral and Santiago became the capital of the kingdom of Galicia. The town was fortified in the 11th century after suffering attacks from the Muslims of Al Andalus. Santiago's rich architectural heritage demonstrates its role as the most important city in Galicia through the ages. Santiago's Old City was designated a UNESCO World Heritage Site in 1985.

Catedral de Santiago

(free, 981569327, 7am-9pm, Pilgrim mass is held daily at 7:30am, 9:30am, noon and 7:30pm in Spanish, English mass at 10:30am at pilgrim office chapel). Pilgrims first head to the **Praza de Obradoiro**, the large open plaza facing the iconic western façade of the cathedral (featured on the euro coins €.05, €.02 and €.01). Medieval pilgrims gathered here and spent their first night in the city keeping vigil in the plaza or inside at the high altar. Pilgrims would then attend Mass and receive indulgences and make their offerings to Santiago and the chapels of other saints. The pilgrim would confess to a priest and obtain their **Compostela**. Today you'll have to walk to the pilgrim office to receive yours. Due to the high number of pilgrims, the office now issues tickets with a number and QR code that directs you to a website where you can monitor the wait.

Cathedral Museum: (€10 for pilgrims, 902557812, Tues-Sat 10am-2pm 4-7pm, Sun 10am-2pm Mon closed) One ticket gets you into the museum permanent collection, Portico de la Gloria, Palacio de Gelmírez and temporary exhibits.

Hostal de los Reyes Católicas: To the L when facing the cathedral from Praza do Obradoiro is the sumptuous Hostal de los Reyes Católicas, a 1501 pilgrim hospital commissioned by Ferdinand and Isabella, the *Reyes Católicas* ("Catholic monarchs"). The building served as hostel, infirmary, and orphanage. Under Franco, the splendid historic building with its Plateresque door was converted into a Parador, one of a series of luxury hotels throughout Spain using historic buildings.

† Monasterio de San Martín Pinario (981-574502)
Just north of the cathedral off Praza do Imaculada is the impressive Monasterio de San Martín Pinario. The Baroque façade is organized like a retablo and features an interesting staircase. The retablo mayor is very fine Baroque including images of

ARCA TO SANTIAGO DE COMPOSTELA

Santiago. The ornate *Churrigueresque* altarpiece shows San Martín riding alongside St. James. Part of the monastery serves as accommodations, with good value pilgrim rooms.

🏛 **Museo das Peregrinacións** (Pilgrimage Museum, free, ⏰Tu-F 9:30am-8pm, Sa 11am-7:30pm, Su 10:15-2:45pm, *Rúa de San Miguel 4*, ☎981-581558 📧) Interesting museum dedicated to the Santiago pilgrimage. The museum has a new exhibit at *Praza Praterías 2* including a cathedral model and an interactive video game where you can role-play a medieval pilgrim.

🏛 **Museo do Pobo Galego** (Museum of the Galician People, free, ⏰Tu-Sa 10am-2pm and 4-7:30pm, Su 11am-3pm, *San Domingos de Bonaval*, ☎981-583620 📧) This museum features artifacts from Galician history as far back as Celtic times, displayed in a 14th-century convent (Santo Domingo de Bonaval). The museum includes a Gothic chapel where several famous Galicians are entombed.

🏛 **Centro Galego de Arte Contemparánea** (Galician Center of Contemporary Art, free, ⏰summer Tu-Su 12pm-9pm, winter Tu-Su 11am-8pm, *Rúa Ramón María del Valle Inclán*, ☎981-546619 📧) Next to the Museo do Pobo Galego, this modern art museum shows a contemporary window into Galician life with high-quality exhibits.

Transportation from Santiago

✈ **Santiago de Compostela Airport** (SCQ) is located in Lavacolla, about 15km outside of Santiago. **City bus 6A** has direct buses from Hórreo bus stop to the airport every ~40 min: 7:20am-10pm (€1, 30 min, Tralusa Co ☎981581815 📧). A **private taxi** to the airport costs €23. Numerous airlines offer inexpensive flights to major European cities.

🚆 **Santiago's train station** (*Rúa do Hórreo 75*, ☎902-240202) connects to most major city in Spain. The high speed *AVE* train to Madrid takes only 3 hours. Information at Renfe 📧

🚌 **Santiago's bus station** (*Rúa Clara Campoamor*, ☎981-542416) connects to most of the major hubs of Spain via **Alsa** and **Monbus** companies 📧, just south of the train station.

CAMINO DE SANTIAGO: CAMINO FRANCÉS

About the Authors

The authors with their children in Dolly Sods, West Virginia.

Anna Dintaman and **David Landis** are the cofounders of Village to Village Press and bring over 15 years of experience working with walking and cycling routes in Europe, the Middle East and Asia, as well as in their home area in the Shenandoah Valley of Virginia. Both are avid hikers and cyclists, with experiences ranging from backpacking Patagonia and Nepal, to hiking in the Middle East and biking across the USA. David cofounded the Jesus Trail, a hiking trail that connects sites from the life of Jesus and developed the TransVirginia gravel bikepacking route.

They have shared a deep love for the Camino since they each first took a 500-mile journey on the Camino Francés in 2009. They enjoy introducing their children to the joys of walking, the outdoors, and learning from other cultures.

Feedback welcome: info@villagetovillagepress.com

facebook.com/caminoguidebooks
instagram.com/caminoguidebook

Village to Village Press specializes in publishing guidebooks and supporting trail development projects worldwide.

CaminoGuidebook.com
Visit for free planning information including easy online booking, digital interactive maps, GPS tracks for navigation and frequently asked questions.

Kindle versions also available

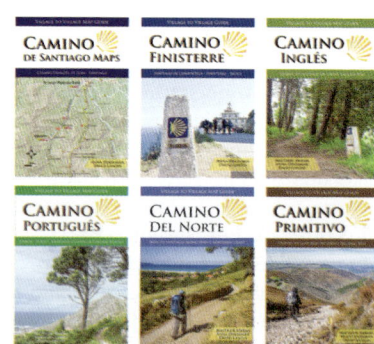